It's Personal: The Art of Building Your Practice

2nd Edition

Andrea T. Eliscu. BS, RN

Medical Group Management Association
104 Inverness Terrace East
Englewood, CO 80112-5306
877.275.6462
mgma.org

Medical Group Management Association®

Library of Congress Cataloging-in-Publication Data
Eliscu, Andrea; author
MGMA (Association); publisher.
EGZ Publications; production.
It's Personal: The Art of Building your Practice
  p ; cm
Includes bibliographical references and index.

Description: 2nd. | Englewood, CO : Medical Group Management Association,
   [2016] | Preceded by: A+ Marketing: Proven Tactics forSuccess / Andrea Eliscu.
   c2008. | Includes bibliographical references and index.

Subjects: 1. Medical care-U.S.-Marketing 2. Medicine-Practice-U.S.-Management
[DNLM 1. Marketing of Health Services-Methods-U.S. 2. Practice Management,
Medical-U.S. 3. Public Relations-U.S. W 74 AA1 E43a 2008]
RA410.56.E36 2008
362.1068'8--dc22

MGMA product id 9036/e9036

PRINT ISBN 978-1-56829-527-5
DIGITAL ISBN 978-1-56829-526-7

Printed in the United States of America
10 9 8 7 6 5 4 3 2 1

Acknowledgements

I feel truly blessed. It's not often that one has the opportunity to tell his or her story to friends, colleagues and those eager to begin their healthcare marketing journey. I've now had that experience four times due in part to my wonderful team, who encourages me, and lends their support and expertise to accomplish it.

I thank each one of you, with special thanks to: Richard J. Walsh, Marlon McClain, Meg Crofton, Bob Kodzis and Debbie Muse.

I also want to recognize the incredible, creative work of our Web site development, graphic design, videography and photography partners: Jay Rieckmann, Susan Rieckmann, and Marcus Burnette at Thrive Creative; Ramona Hacker; Ted Gonzalez; Courtney Shapiro; and the dynamic duo of Marc Middleton and Bill Shafer at Growing Bolder.

This book would not be a useful teaching tool without the wonderful clients and professionals who graciously allowed me to share examples of their leadership and marketing work: Dennis Buhring, Linda Zinkovich, Jeff Brockette, Fran Crawford, Charles May, Allan Sansom, Len Allison, Michelle Foster, Mo Azam, MD, Anand Patel, MD, Robert Masson, MD, and David Auerbach, DO.

I'd also like to say a special thanks to my late husband, Edward H. Eliscu, MD, who shared his vision, support, and understanding of the healthcare community and its changing ways, even as he traveled on his own journey.

And finally, I want to thank the visionary and supportive team at MGMA. They were champions in encouraging me to update this book. Special thanks to Craig Wiberg, MLS, MBA, MGMA's senior product manager, who gave me the opportunity to share my knowledge and experience with MGMA's audience.

Contents

Introduction

As I prepared to write this book, I reflected back on my 30-plus years of advising physicians about how to market their practices. And while the Healthcare industry has seen enormous change, I believe that the old adage, "the more things change, the more they stay the same," rings truer than ever before when it comes to the fundamentals of effective medical marketing.

Those of you practicing medicine or managing a healthcare practice or organization grapple with changes and challenges every day, and no doubt the list can seem daunting:

- Patient-centered medical homes
- Accountable care organizations
- Team-based care
- Bundled payments
- Value-based purchasing
- Patient outcomes and satisfaction
- An aging population
- Chronic care management
- Payer mergers/consolidation
- Meaningful use standards
- Data security and HIPAA compliance
- Telemedicine and virtual visits

Payment models are shifting, government mandates are increasing, patients are becoming more empowered, and physicians want to control their own destinies. These challenges can create confusion and uncertainty, but I believe they also provide opportunity for those physicians and medical practices willing to lead. I also believe, because of all of these factors, that medical marketing has taken on a more important role than ever before.

Medical marketing was an almost novel concept 30 years ago. Most practices at the time were very reluctant to take such a drastic step. But when a brave physician or practice manager was convinced to make the revolutionary decision to market the group, three basic steps became essential to the process, and those steps remain the same today:

1. Practice quality medicine,

2. Develop a brand-name identity, and

3. Focus on patient/customer service.

In my three previous books published by Medical Group Management Association (MGMA)—*Position for Success: Strategic Marketing for Group Practices*, *Ready-Set-Market!* and *A+ Marketing: Proven Tactics for Success*—I covered these fundamentals along with the rationale for marketing, how to "think" marketing, and how to set and achieve specific marketing goals. I also presented several case studies to illustrate the basics. These fundamentals have stood the test of time. Only the specific strategies used to achieve your goals have evolved and changed.

What physicians once resisted—marketing and communicating to meet the needs of their patients/customers—has now become an important part of everyday business. Instead of a bold move on the part of a medical practice, marketing is virtually a necessity today to establish and maintain a successful practice. In fact, given the list of challenges I detailed above, #3: Focus on patient/customer service, has become more important than ever before.

THE RISE OF THE "PROSUMER"

Over the past 30 years, not only has healthcare changed, patients have changed, too. They are better educated, better informed and more inclined to take control of their own healthcare, especially as they increasingly carry more of the financial burden. We have evolved from a physician-directed model to a patient-driven one.

Patients have become "prosumers". They are proactive before consuming. They read, research, talk, surf and chat online to gather information before making decisions, including those about their healthcare.

So practicing medicine today means viewing a patient not just as someone who is ill and needs your help, but as a consumer making a purchasing decision—that decision just happens to be related to the health and well-being of themselves or a loved one. And as the most successful businesses in other industries already know, the customer should always be your number one priority.

In addition, these prosumers come to your practice armed with mounds of information they have gathered from the internet (some accurate, some not), and they demand answers and service like never before. Although some physicians may find this troubling, realize that these well-educated patients are likely to be more compliant, which will likely contribute to better outcomes.

And that's what we're all working toward, isn't it? Patients engaged in their Healthcare who proactively work with their doctors to resolve any issues.

HOW TO USE THIS BOOK

My goal for this book is simple. I want to provide an easy, practical how-to guide that will help you, a practice administrator or a physician manager, understand the importance of marketing, build the right foundation for the goals and projects you want to accomplish, and prepare the tools that you need to implement them. These are the roadmaps to success for you and your patients/customers. The ideas I present are things that you and the practice can implement on your own with minimal assistance.

And please note that while I have used the words "customers" and "patients" interchangeably, customers do comprise populations beyond patients, such as referrers, internal staff, community leaders, vendors and others.

I've included examples of action plans and other materials from different types of group practices across the United States. I've tried to illustrate how you can put these strategies to work and how they might look in your practice. You may also note that I say similar things in different ways in different chapters. This is primarily for emphasis but also to illustrate multiple points where certain goals, objectives or strategies may apply.

I hope you find my book a user-friendly marketing tool, and I hope you find my recommendations easy to implement in your practice.

So let's get started. The first step is to decide what you want to achieve. After you know your goals, you can take charge of your dream, investigate how to attain it, and finally achieve everything you want based on your available budget.

Good luck!

CHAPTER 1

From the 4 P's to the 4 A's

Any basic business marketing book or course will talk about the "four P's"—product, price, place and promotion. These elements are still the building blocks of any successful enterprise. However, what today's prosumers believe they want, deserve and expect has become the driving force in healthcare purchasing decisions.

Service has become an increasingly important part of the "product" physicians provide. Healthcare has become a highly competitive marketplace, and that competitiveness will only increase. You can have stellar credentials and provide the highest level of medical care available, but if you can't keep your patients happy, many will leave and find someone who will.

The cornerstone to any physician's survival and success is what I call the **"Four A's:"**

* **Access**

* **Availability**

* **Accountability**

* **Accommodation**

The Four A's are today's new customer service issues. They include everything that makes marketing a practice successful and they're highly interrelated. There are times when **Access** and **Availability** seem to be the same, and there are times when **Accommodation** is really about **Availability** and **Access**. Let's break them down.

1

ACCESS

Patients want the highest level of care when they need it, where they need it. They want the freedom to choose and be involved in decisions about their care. Access is the primary reason behind the explosion in walk-in clinics. These businesses have capitalized on the fact that many patients could not get access to their regular physicians in a time they felt was reasonable. And these businesses are booming. While most patients would prefer to see their personal physician, they are often willing to give this up in exchange for access to care.

So, how can you increase **Access**?

One pediatric practice I work with developed a "Fast Track" service for three hours every weekday morning, providing guaranteed walk-in care for their patients. This same practice also opened a second office in a neighboring community not so much to attract new patients, but to better serve their current patients. They realized that an increasing number of their patients were driving over a bridge across county lines to reach their practice. Unfortunately, that 10-mile trip would often take 30 minutes or more thanks to interstate traffic. So, after listening to their patients, the practice opened a new, full-time community office, in the neighboring county, allowing them to increase patient satisfaction while also boosting new patient referrals from their existing patient base.

Another aspect of access involves the time and quality of the interactions patients have with their physician or healthcare provider. Do you allow patients ample time to discuss their concerns and ask questions when they are in the office? Do you involve them in decisions about their care? How do you provide them access to information once they are home and think of additional questions? Your website can be invaluable in this regard. It should be more than just a brochure promoting your practice. It should also be an interactive resource and tool to educate, engage and serve your current patients.

AVAILABILITY

Do you offer convenient appointment times?

How long do your patients typically wait both to secure an appointment and in the office?

Are your physicians and staff approachable and easy to talk to?

Do they handle phone calls in an unhurried and compassionate manner?

Offering non-traditional appointment times may not be a new idea, but it is certainly one whose time has come. Our world no longer operates on the nine-to-five day it once did. Increasingly, thanks in large part to technology, we live in a 24/7 world, and as a result, today's prosumers need and expect additional availability.

No one expects you to put up the "Open 24 hours" sign—although it might be appreciated. However, many forward-thinking medical practices now offer non-traditional appointment times—early in the morning, at lunchtime, early evening and even Saturdays—based on the specific needs of their patient population. And still others are exploring telemedicine and virtual visits.

Know your patient base. Does your practice serve a large number of professionals who need an appointment on their way to or home from work or on their lunch break? Or do you serve a large senior population that doesn't want to be on the road during rush hour? Do you have a large number of pediatric patients who need to be seen after school hours or on the weekend? Does your scheduling reflect these needs?

Many of the practices I have worked with have successfully implemented non-traditional appointment times and service, increasing their patients' satisfaction without increasing individual physician or staff hours. It just takes creativity and flexibility, and often some surveying and experimenting to determine the exact formula that works best for you.

ACCOUNTABILITY

The buck stops here.

Patients want someone who will take responsibility and provide them with accurate answers and explanations. Typically, they are already anxious and under stress when they turn to you. They are probably experiencing a health problem. They have questions and concerns and are looking to you and your staff for answers. They don't want to get passed from one person to another. They expect leadership, assistance and guidance in navigating what can be a complex healthcare maze.

One example of how healthcare providers are addressing the need for accountability is the rise in care coordinators or care teams. This approach provides each patient with a single point person who handles all questions and issues related to his/her care. And it also helps put patients at ease because they see the same familiar face and hear the same familiar voice each time they interact with the office. By doing this, you are building relationships and loyalty by providing a more personal level of care. This can make even large, impersonal, multi-physician or multi-specialty practices feel personal.

Think about it. When times are tough, we all want someone we can turn to and depend on. No excuses. Just action.

ACCOMMODATION

Today's prosumer patients expect that you will accommodate them. They want convenience and to feel a genuine concern for their well-being—someone who understands their unique, individual challenges and makes it easy to get the personalized care they need. They don't want cookie-cutter care. They want customization. They want to feel engaged and personally recognized during the time they are connected with your practice.

So with all the demands on your practice, how can you take the time to provide more customized care? It's less a matter of time than an attitude of consideration and thoughtfulness.

For example, if you are late and make a patient wait (which does inevitably happen), how do you and your staff handle the situation? Does someone come out and explain the situation to the patient and keep them updated? I often don't mind waiting if I know my doctor had to spend extra time with another patient due to an emergency or urgent need, especially if I feel I can expect the same should I ever need it. But I can't accept waiting with no acknowledgement of my needs or the value of my time, no explanation of why I am waiting, or no indication of how long it might be.

Do you offer to reschedule? Do you personally apologize? Did someone offer the patient something—like a $5 gift card to a neighboring business—to grab a sandwich or a cup of coffee? Do you offer Wi-Fi so patients can work or take care of other responsibilities while they wait? If it turns out to be an extensive delay, do you try to reach them before they even come in?

WHY THE 4 A'S?

In today's business environment—and medicine today is absolutely a business—all the marketing in the world won't equal success if you forget that your customers are your number one priority. Simply put: if you don't keep them happy, they'll find someone who will. And it's easier than ever today to change when healthcare is being delivered by publicly traded companies at locations right in your community.

Families can now receive healthcare at Super Wal-Mart, Walgreen's, CVS Pharmacy, and even in grocery stores. Those patients are willing to accept what might be considered a lower (or at least different) quality of care in exchange for having **Access, Availability, Accommodation,** and someone who will accept **Accountability**.

NOW TAKE ACTION

Ready to take action and incorporate the 4 A's—**Access, Availability, Accountability** and **Accommodation**—into your practice? Start by spending some time walking in your patient's footsteps. What do they need? What do they want? What do they value most? What do they like and dislike about your practice? Ask your staff to do the same and gather everyone's thoughts and ideas. Then, take a step back and examine your current systems, identify potential opportunities and be sure to engage your staff in developing creative solutions to become an A+ practice.

CHAPTER 2

The Power of the Basics—
A Few Important Points

Far from being a novel concept, medical marketing today is a subject discussed in scores of books, including the three I've written previously for MGMA. But let's go over several important elements that you must understand and utilize if your marketing program is to succeed. Primarily, I want you to understand that marketing means meeting the needs of your customers, and I want to empower you to take charge of your practice.

My aim for this book is to present information that will both help you develop the specific goals you want to achieve and develop a plan of action to achieve these goals. When you review your plan 12 months from now, I want you to see that you've made real progress. Toward that aim, I'll also present practical marketing opportunities that you can easily implement within your practice.

As you proceed, keep in mind my cornerstones of physician practice marketing: **The Four A's—Access, Availability, Accountability**, and **Accommodation**.

As you plan your strategies and tactics, ask these questions at each step:

- As our practice initiates this marketing plan of action, which of these four cornerstones have we addressed?
  - Will this marketing project allow **Access** for our customers?
  - Will we be **Available** to our patients?
  - Will our staff, both professional and clerical, be **Accountable**?
  - And can we **Accommodate** our customers?

7

Traditionally, two of the methods used to measure a service organization's success were timeliness and accuracy. Now with The Four A's, we have opportunities for additional measurements to consider in meeting our clients' needs.

Remember, it's pointless to spend creative energy and financial resources without first being in touch with your target markets and their needs. Without that information, you will never achieve your desired outcome.

BUILDING YOUR PRACTICE IDENTITY

I won't be delving deep into the basics, though there is one very specific, fundamental element of marketing that I do want to talk about: the necessity to build brand-name identity, which I believe is a vital element of customer service.

You must establish and build your brand name—a.k.a. your practice identity—within your community (or multiple communities if you have multiple community offices). And I strongly encourage you to use the term community offices rather than satellite offices. The latter term connotes something of lesser quality or status than the "primary office," whereas the former indicates a service, an outreach to serve a community through enhanced Access and convenience. It's just as easy to refer to your community offices based on their locations.

Building brand-name identity, or managing your brand, is a promise to deliver a healthcare experience for your patients that is specific and unique to your practice. You're essentially making a promise no one else can make; it's the essence of how your practice delivers healthcare and service. It requires that you recognize what patients want, both in the delivery of care and their emotional relationships with your practice. A key part of this process is conducting a gap analysis that involves identifying what you can do and can't do compared to your competitors. What you do the same as your competitors is just as important as what you do better and what you don't do.

To build brand-name identity, you first must determine who you are and how you want to be perceived by your customers. Whether your customers are patients, referring physicians, employers, insurance companies, or internal staff—or often some combination. Whatever the case, you must know what you stand for as well as understand your practice focus and your service commitment. And you must communicate this to your customers.

If you don't define yourself, other practices within your specialty will do it for you. And you don't want that to happen. A marketing planning retreat, while not vital, can be a valuable way to accomplish this.

DEVELOPING YOUR ACTION PLAN

Developing a comprehensive strategic marketing plan can be an invaluable tool for your practice, though it takes time and commitment. The plan can take various forms, but typically contains the following core elements:

- **Background/Situational Analysis**—Describe your current situation. Are there specific changes or challenges within your practice that have led you to develop a plan? Are there things on the horizon that will impact your practice (i.e., a physician retiring, a new physician joining the practice, a new service/procedure, payer changes, increased competition in the market, etc.). Detailing these items will help frame your work and the focus of the rest of your plan.

- **Goals/Objectives**—Develop three to five key objectives you want to accomplish and make sure they are measurable.

- **Target Audiences**—Who is the primary audience you need to reach with your message? Are there secondary audiences you should also consider? Detail who each of these groups are and what they "look" like—where they live/work, age, health condition, specialty if they are a physician, etc.

- **SWOT Analysis**—SWOT stands for Strengths, Weaknesses, Opportunities and Threats. This is one of the most valuable exercises in developing your plan. Involve your team and be completely truthful. Put a mirror on your practice. It can also be helpful to have the perspective and input of those outside your group. Use your patient survey feedback. Interview several referral sources. Understanding your strengths, weaknesses, opportunities and threats, and then addressing them head on, is one of the best ways to bridge any gaps and elevate your brand.

- **Competitive Analysis**—Identify your primary competitors and their brand positioning within the community. What are their strengths? What are their weaknesses? What message are they sending? How do you compare?

- **Key Messages**—Based on all of the items detailed above, determine what it is you want your target audience to know. What makes you different? What makes you strong? What makes you unique and valuable? How do you meet their needs or fill a gap?

* **Strategies/Tactics**—These are the specific projects or action items you will take on to accomplish your goals. Some are basic and standard practice to deliver on your service promise. Others can be creative and create lasting impressions that help you to stand out from the crowd.

See Exhibits 2.1 and 2.2 for sample plans that incorporate these elements.

Once the plan is complete, it is time to prioritize and implement. Don't let this plan sit in a binder on a shelf. This is a living, breathing document to use and reference in order to guide your efforts. And to prevent the implementation from becoming too daunting, determine three or four key goals or projects you need or want to accomplish within a year and concentrate all of your efforts on those. This helps enhance your brand-name identity in the marketplace while allowing you to control your level of service to the patients and others using your practice.

**EXHIBIT 2.1 Southern Oregon Orthopedics:
Marketing & Public Relations Action Plan**

Background

Located in Medford, Oregon, Southern Oregon Orthopedics (SOO) is southern Oregon's largest orthopedic surgery group and, since 1970, has served the residents of southern Oregon and northern California. All 12 of their physicians are fellowship-trained, providing surgical care for injuries and illnesses that affect the spine, shoulders, knees, feet, ankles, hips, elbows, hands and wrists. They also serve as the exclusive orthopedic trauma surgeons for both Rogue Valley Medical Center (Asante) and Providence Medford Medical Center, and are supported by a team of physician assistants and nurse practitioners.

The group has been the dominant orthopedic surgery provider in the region with very little competition. However, that is slowly starting to increase with additional orthopedic surgeons moving into the area. Currently, SOO has working relationships with both major hospital systems in their market — Asante and Providence — with some SOO physicians operating exclusively at Asante, some exclusively at Providence, and some who perform cases at both. In addition, SOO physicians perform outpatient procedures in the Surgery Center of Southern Oregon located next door to the practice.

While the group enjoys a strong reputation for quality physicians and superior medical outcomes, the practice faces some service issues in regard to the phone system, wait times, appointment availability and referring physicians. In order to maintain brand integrity and a leadership position in the market, it is important that the practice appear united in its approach with patients, referral sources and the community.

Because SOO has enjoyed a dominant position in the market, the practice has done minimal marketing. In addition, its Website, while it contains a considerable amount of content, appears dated in design and structure. It does not accurately reflect the desired brand/image of the practice as a strong, cohesive, sophisticated, service-oriented, patient-focused leader in the field of orthopedics and in the Rogue Valley community.

SOO needs to cement its brand (includes service provided to patients and referral sources) in the marketplace to proactively counteract any increased competition and maintain a leadership position.

Practice Goals

- Preserve "independent" practice style and control destiny through contracting and growth.
- Develop, strengthen and solidify relationships with key referral sources.
- Grow and diversify the referral base to attract new referral sources and patients to the practice.
- Establish Southern Oregon Orthopedics as the orthopedic thought leaders among the Southern Oregon healthcare and executive/employer market.
- Retain and attract patients by providing the highest level of service among orthopedic practices in the Southern Oregon market.

continued

EXHIBIT 2.1 Southern Oregon Orthopedics: Marketing & Public Relations Action Plan

continued

Target Audience

- Referring Physicians:
    - Primary Care — Family Medicine, Internal Medicine, Pediatrics;
    - Urgent Care.
- Physical and Occupational Therapists;
- Hospitals/Local Healthcare Leaders;
- Chiropractors;
- Consumers in the Rogue Valley — especially surgical candidates, ages 18-62, with commercial insurance and low BMI;
- Sports Market — high schools, local sports organizations/events/venues;
- Local Executives/Major Employers.

Strengths

- Caliber and breadth of physicians in the practice (experienced, fellowship-trained, sub-specialized) — some perform highly technical surgeries that others in the area do not.
- Size of group — largest in the market, "one-stop shop" for orthopedic care.
- Overall quality of patient medical care provided (outcomes), including access to the latest clinical techniques.
- Longevity in the market (serving Southern Oregon and Northern California since 1970);
- Facility;
- On-site PT and OT;
- On-site MRI, x-ray, fluoroscan, ultrasound;
- Team of nurse practitioners to help facilitate rapid assessment of patients;
- Sports Injury Line — provides direct access;
- Surgery center next door.

Weaknesses

- Lack of group orientation to achieve goals. Don't always appear as a united front/cohesive unit to the community.
- Communication with referring physicians.
- Don't accurately track source of referrals.
- At times, availability/expediency in getting in for an appointment (especially for urgent care/worker's comp referrals.)
- Patient office wait times.
- Lack of patient education materials/instructions.

continued

**EXHIBIT 2.1 Southern Oregon Orthopedics:
Marketing & Public Relations Action Plan**

continued

Weaknesses (cont.)

- Phone system — includes answering and returning calls.
- Lack of after-hours/weekend care.
- Service provided by front office staff.
- Sports medicine community outreach is driven by just one person.
- Logo and printed materials look dated.
- SOO name and logo not on the building.

Opportunities

- Entrench as the dominant leader in orthopedics in the region and grow to maintain that dominance.
- Operate more effectively as a group with a focus on "patient first."
- Be more collaborative with referring physicians — improve outreach/communication/ education, thank-you/appreciation.
- Formalize sports medicine protocols and consider expanding program.
- Educate patients about role of physician assistants and nurse practitioners.
- Enhance patient experience through better education materials.
- Build more brand awareness/general visibility in the community.
- Expand to outlying communities.
- Add additional physicians to meet patient demand.
- Be more proactive to changes in the market.

Threats/Challenges

- Increasing competition.
- Getting patients into and through the system in an efficient manner with good physician and staff rapport.
- Space within current office.

Primary Competitors

- Four orthopedic competitors. Additional competition from local neurosurgeons and podiatrists for back/spine and foot/ankle.

Key Messages

Current tag lines include:

- "Our Specialty is You!"
- "The Experts in Sports Medicine" (for sports medicine marketing in the schools and community.)

continued

EXHIBIT 2.1 Southern Oregon Orthopedics: Marketing & Public Relations Action Plan

continued

Key Messages(cont.)

Messaging should focus on providing a full range of the highest level of specialized orthopedic care while also emphasizing service and caring:

- The area's largest, most experienced orthopedic practice, serving Southern Oregon and Northern California since 1970

- Access to a team of 12 board-certified, fellowship-trained physicians sub-specialized in sports medicine, joint replacement, spine, foot and ankle, and hand.

- Can develop a list of "firsts." Examples include:

  - First fellowship-trained orthopedist in Rogue Valley

  - First in the area to perform arthroscopic ligament repairs in the knee and shoulder

  - First in Oregon to do outpatient partial knee replacements

PHASE 1: SOLIDIFY INFRASTRUCTURE AND SERVICE

Strategy	Notes
Logo	
Develop a new logo and corporate identity package (includes letter-head, envelopes, business and appt. cards, note card and envelope.)	The design and colors of your logo and current corporate identity materials (rusty brown on cream paper) look mid-80s. Need an updated logo that reinforces your brand as strong in 2015 and beyond, and visually communicates your position as a modern, sophisticated, service-oriented, patient-focused leader in the field of orthopedics and in the Rogue Valley community. New logo needs to be placed on outside of building. All practice printed materials should be branded with the new logo. Note card will become a key marketing tool for referral development/thank-you's, etc.
Marketing 101 Presentation	
Hold a meeting with all of the physicians to share this approach to marketing.	This is critical to ensure support and engagement as you proceed with the marketing plan.
Service Patient Experience/Patient Communication	
Continue an ongoing patient satisfaction survey.	It is important that the results are monitored and responded to directly if possible and in a timely manner. This is critical as you work to move the needle on the concerns and issues already identified.

continued

PHASE 1: SOLIDIFY INFRASTRUCTURE AND SERVICE

Strategy	Notes
Service/Patient Experience/Patient Communication	*continued*

Strategy	Notes
Establish customer service standards for answering phones, on hold wait time, returning calls, access to appointments, office wait time, etc.	Create benchmarks to measure improvement.
Conduct customer service training for all schedulers and office staff.	Goal is to ensure the service provided to patients is of the highest quality possible. This is a big part of your brand.
Understanding the Source(s) of Your New Patients Consider incorporating a brief — "Where Have You Seen Us?" or "How Did You Hear About Us?" — survey into your new patient communication/visit.	It is helpful to get a sense of what marketing/community efforts might be working best. Also provides an opportunity to capture and then send personal thank you's to top referrers (whether patients, other community members or physicians.)
Ensure that your office reflects your brand and has personality: • Name/new logo in waiting room; • Names/photos of staff in waiting room (make them personal/different from your typical headshot); • Updated patient educational materials; • Consider rotating monthly information board in waiting room (highlight different timely orthopedic topics); • Personal artwork/photography.	Create a warm, inviting, soothing, healing, patient-friendly environment. Consider framed photography of active/outdoor lifestyle around Southern Oregon. May even want to have a "wall of fame" where photos of past patients back in their sport/hobby/active lifestyle can be decoratively framed and displayed if they wish. Also discussed adding TVs to waiting room to share ortho health information (could also run SOO patient testimonials and physician bio videos once complete.)
Identify all of your patient touchpoints and develop/research new ways to overdeliver. Examples: • Give a gift card to a patient who experiences an excessive wait. Be prompt with patient requests. • Streamline paperwork/process for obtaining patient info/updates. • Minimize cancellations. • Provide personal attention—great patient by name, track and remember/mention something about each patient (i.e. a sports hobby, children, etc.—something they shared at their last visit.) • Call patients within a few days after the first visit or surgery to follow up and check on them. • When running late, allow patient time/place to make a phone call (to office, babysitter, etc.) • If running late, offer coffee or water, or during lunch hour appointments, offer to order lunch to-go for patient from previously identified nearby café/deli (keep menu on hand.)	This can be a great team-building exercise with your office staff/leaders. Examples of touchpoints: calling the office, scheduling an appointment, meeting the receptionist, waiting in the waiting room, waiting in an exam room, meeting the nurse, meeting the physician, obtaining test results, calling with a question, receiving a bill, etc.) Steps: 1. Identify all current touchpoints. 2. Work with staff to determine current approach. 3. Develop creative ideas to "overdeliver" on each one. 4. Compile suggestions and present to physician partners. 5. Implement as appropriate.
Create name badges for each staff person w/ your new updated logo. Should include first name, last initial, and hometown.	Makes them personal. Hometown can help spark connections and conversation with patients, helping to put them at ease.

PHASE 1: SOLIDIFY INFRASTRUCTURE AND SERVICE

Strategy	Notes
Service/Patient Experience/Patient Communication	*continued*
Create a nice sign/plaque for your waiting rooms with "your commitment/promise to your patients."	
Establish a formal staff orientation process for all new staff. Cover your vision, the history of the practice, educate about all services, discuss patient flow and referring physician protocol.	Ensure that everyone who works for you is a good "spokesperson" for the practice and can cross market your various services in the community
Consider adding a few more handicap parking spaces.	We noticed this was mentioned several times on your patient satisfaction surveys. As an orthopedic practice, providing easy access is critical to the patient experience.
Create a fact sheet to educate patients on the role of PAs and NPs in your practice—position them as leaders/experts in their areas.	Things you can put on fact sheet template: As you continue to use and rely more upon physician extenders, it is important to educate patients on the extenders' roles, qualifications, and experience. Be sure to share this piece with your referral sources so they can provide patients when a referral is made. Also include the fact sheet on your website!
Referral Protocol, Communication and Tracking	
Consider establishing an internal referral manager/coordinator to help oversee physician referrals and make sure no communication falls between the cracks.	Let referral offices know this is a point person (provide cell #) in case they have any issues. Proactively visit/communicate with referring docs offices to let them know protocol, etc. Ensure referring docs are receiving medical notes back on the patient care.
Develop a monthly report that tracks referrals by source (physicians, PT, chiropractors, self referrals, etc.) • Be sure to include practice/group name as well as a referring physician's name if it is a physician referral. • Create a 90-day report to look at referral trends. • Develop a plan to respond immediately if you notice referrals from a particular source slowing or drying up.	
Based on data above, stratify your referral sources into 3 groups: 1. Top Referrers (most loyal); 2. Somewhat Regular Referrers; 3. Low Referrers - In this group, need to determine if there are any who should be referring more and create a list of who to target.	

continued

PHASE 1: SOLIDIFY INFRASTRUCTURE AND SERVICE

Strategy	Notes
Referral Protocal, Communication and Tracking	*continued*
Capture email addresses for all referral sources.	This allows you to more easily communicate updates if needed.
Develop an annual referral source survey.	Need to determine best way to facilitate (email w/ on-line link like Survey Monkey, by phone, or in person). Should be brief—no more than 5 questions. Purpose is to measure progress on service to referral sources and identify any gaps/opportunities.
Develop referral protocol—a turn-key system for how all referrals will be handled.	Consider dedicated referral phone #/coordinator(s) as mentioned above.
• When you have received a referral from a new referral source, call and/or send a personalized thank-you to the referral source right away (within 24-48 hours.) If it is a physician referral, this thank-you should be in addition to sending any patients' medical notes/reports. • Determine patient referral access time (i.e., within 1 week.) • Review policies/systems for communicating with referring physicians throughout the time their patients are in your care. Ensure that you are being as service-oriented as possible. Commit to report turn-around time. • Review communication that occurs when a patient is discharged back to a referring physician (i.e., thank them again for trusting their patient to your care, instructions for any follow-up, concerns, things to watch/look for, etc.)	It is key to make communication with referral sources as warm and personal as possible. While clinical reports are important, you also want to nurture the relationship and stand out from any competitors. Be sure to send thank-you notes to non-physician referral sources as well (i.e., physical therapists, etc.) If referred by another patient, also send a thank-you note, just be sure to keep it generic ("Thank you so much for referring to my practice. I appreciate and value your confidence in me....") so as not to mention the new patient's name and violate any privacy rules. For ongoing referral sources, don't need to send a personal thank-you every time, but recommend sending a personal note periodically just to reinforce the relationship and show your appreciation.
Develop a mechanism to summarize and respond to any physician-to-physician contacts that focus on dissatisfaction or super-satisfaction in working with your practice.	
If appropriate and helpful for your work flow, create pre-printed referral pads for current and potential referring docs.	Similar to a prescription pad. Referring physician can simply fill it out, tear off and hand to the patient or to their referral coordinator. Can distribute the pads through personal visits. Create online referral form for your website as well.

continued

PHASE 1: SOLIDIFY INFRASTRUCTURE AND SERVICE

Strategy	Notes
Referral Protocol, Communication and Tracking	*continued*
Develop a plan for regular follow-up/communication with your referring physicians.	Could be coordinated by new referral manager. However, physicians must be personally involved.
• Follow up with each A-list referrer quarterly (can be a phone call, e-mail, handwritten note, cup of coffee, lunch, dinner, community event, etc.)	Can script out various messages for physicians to use on calls or hand-written notes.
• Follow up with each B-list referrer at least twice a year.	You can also have your docs invite key referring docs to join them at a community event (i.e. Britt Festival, sporting event, etc.)
• Develop a targeted strategy to call or meet with each of the C-list sources you want to increase referrals from. After the call or meeting, send a personal, handwritten follow-up note thanking them for their time and detailing how you will work with them to meet their needs and those of their patients. Be sure to address any specific questions or concerns they may have had.	
Letter to Referring Physicians about Service Improvements.	Once you have implemented some service improvements and tracked to ensure the patient experience is indeed enhanced, we recommend sending a letter to your referring providers to let them know. "We've listened, and we've improved to better serve you and your patients ..." Then outline the specific steps you have taken. Could also highlight any key service stats (i.e. reduced wait times by X%, etc.)
Testimonials	
Patient Testimonials—Need to screen, interview and develop written and video testimonials for a number of patients who mirror your ideal target market (at least one for each sub-specialty.) They can talk about their experience and how they have been able to get back to their active lifestyle.	Once completed, these can be used on the Website. Also need to encourage participants to share their story and push it out through their own social media channels, contacts (i.e. Facebook, Twitter, publications, etc.) May also consider using some of these stories/testimonials as part of any advertising. Also try to highlight a patient who has traveled to the practice from outside the immediate area because of your expertise.

continued

PHASE 1: SOLIDIFY INFRASTRUCTURE AND SERVICE

Strategy	Notes
Testimonials	*continued*
Consider developing a few physician quotes/testimonials from those who are top referrers.	Do you have any referring physicians you have treated as patients? This is even better.
	Once again, would need to secure their permission. If planned well in advance, these can be scheduled efficiently in 1 day of shooting to minimize expense.
	Depending on the content, could be used both for marketing to consumers/potential patients as well as referring physicians.
	Could definitely be used in any direct physician communication strategies such as a dedicated physician section of your website. These lend credibility to what you have accomplished and are building—demonstrating your leadership and the respect you have garnered from other doctors.
Printed Marketing Materials	
Need to create a brochure that provides a brief, general overview of the practice.	Need to keep it concise and hit on key messages.
	Provides a general overview of your "story"—practice/vision/services.
	Can serve as a leave-behind for visits to referring docs, community or physician presentations, meetings, discussions, events, etc.
Create printed bio rack cards for each physician.	These should not only include the typical background you would find in a bio but also more personal information like why you chose a career in medicine, what you enjoy most about your specialty, your hobbies and community involvement, etc. Helps people get to know you as a person. Can use these same bios on your website as well.
Develop a Fact Sheet Template.	Using the new logo/branding, create a basic fact sheet template that can be used for any of your patient education fact sheets. Can imprint specific condition/treatment information. Provides uniformity throughout the practice.

continued

PHASE 1: SOLIDIFY INFRASTRUCTURE AND SERVICE

Strategy	Notes
Printed Marketing Materials	*continued*
Develop a "library" of patient education materials.	Some of your physicians make great use of these while others do not. This is an easy way to enhance the patient experience/satisfaction. Recommend that you create a standard set of basic materials for each condition/procedure so that all of your physicians use them. Can be as simple as one sheet. By using the new fact sheet template, they can all easily have a consistent look and style at minimal cost while also being easy to update or change if needed. Also need to develop a system for ensuring these are provided to patients as needed. You may even want to share some of them with referral sources as appropriate. They should mirror the patient education placed on your website. Ideally, you could have them all stored electronically and just print them out as needed. Some electronic health records may even provide this function.
Website/Social Media	
Need to update your webpage design and content to reflect your brand in 2015 and beyond. Need to realign and refresh the content and design to achieve consistency and focus on the benefits provided to patients.	• In general, the site should be more modern and patient-centric. Focus on the benefits to patients more than the features of the practice. • Keep the content clean, concise and easy to navigate. • Add some fresh photography (docs and staff in action, "patients" in action and back to enjoying life. • Consider a page for each subspecialty/center. • Add video patient testimonials. • Explore feasibility of online forms that can be completed and submitted prior to the visit. • Can consider adding logos of the local sports teams you sponsor and work with, which helps to visually demonstrate your commitment to the community. • Could also add a page about all of your community involvement with photos of your docs and staff at events, etc. • Include more patient education on conditions and procedures. • Consider adding a page for referring physicians. Here you can share your referral protocols, include links to your docs' published research, etc.
Place patient testimonials prominently on the homepage of your website and include buttons so it is easy for visitors to your site to share these videos with others via e-mail, Facebook, YouTube, etc. (For example, visit www.jewettortho.com)	

PHASE 1: SOLIDIFY INFRASTRUCTURE AND SERVICE	
Strategy	**Notes**
Website/Social Media	*continued*
Create video bios for all physicians.	These brief videos (2-3 min. max.) highlight you as people (i.e. why you practice medicine, why you chose your specialty, your philosophy of patient care, what you do outside of practicing medicine—hobbies, involvement in sports, children's activities, etc.) They bring your bios to life. For examples, visit www.jewettortho.com and http://www.neurospineinstitute.org
	Also need to be sure to include social media buttons (i.e. e-mail, Facebook, etc.) so it is easy for your website visitors to share these with family and friends.
	As with the patient testimonial videos, these can typically all be shot in one day with enough advanced planning.
Include links on your website to any news articles that highlight/feature you.	This keeps your content fresh, establishes credibility and maximizes your search engine performance.
Need to establish a procedure for addressing online reviews in a timely manner.	Must adhere to HIPAA guidelines while still appearing concerned and responsive. Encouraging patients to write reviews (once customer service issues have been corrected) is another great tactic in that more positive reviews will help to diminish the impact of any negative ones.

PHASE 1: EXTERNAL COMMUNICATION MARKETING	
Reinvigorate the summer block party event.	Many of the physicians we spoke to mentioned this event. Recommend that you give it some renewed focus and energy. Be sure to invite all of your current and potential referral sources as well as neighbors of the practice. All SOO physicians should attend and mingle. It is especially important for the newer, younger physicians. They should make a point to get to know the referring physicians especially. Could you include some type of local entertainment to give it some extra appeal/draw? Also consider hand delivering the invitations (i.e. with a balloon attached or some memorable, fun theming tied to the event).
Begin ongoing referral physician visits—prioritize based on your database/tracking results.	This could be coordinated by the new referral manager. When appropriate, she could bring a physician with her.
Develop a plan to contact new physicians in town who have never referred but should/could. • Call or write a letter of welcome/introduction. Send business card and hand write personal cell phone #. • Make a follow-up personal visit to provide referral pad.	We realize this may be a small group but important nonetheless.

PHASE 2: EXTERNAL COMMUNICATION MARKETING

Strategy	Notes
Referring Physicians	*continued*
Send an inexpensive, personalized gift to all of your A-list referrers sometime other than the holidays.	Be as personal and creative as possible. (i.e. personalized golf/workout towels, unique fishing fly, portable cell phone charger, etc.)
In lieu of the typical holiday gift, develop a strategy to creatively thank all of your referring physicians. Consider a donation in their honor to a local cause/ charity.	Some nonprofit organizations will send a note to each of your referring docs letting them know a gift was made in their honor.
Thank the staff of your top referral sources annually. Consider doing something for one-two offices each month (depending on how many you have). Send an appropriate gift or have some of your staff take their staff to lunch or bring lunch to them.	Also consider thanking surgery center and hospital surgical staffs.
Look into providing a CME at Providence.	Perhaps a few of your younger physicians could do this talk together to highlight differences among the sub-specialties.
Jefferson Health Information Exchange	Continue involvement in this group.
Advertising	
Continue NPR Rhythm & News sponsorship.	Recommend continuing this sponsorship and perhaps even expanding it as appropriate to reach some of the outlying areas. Also need to change the message at least quarterly to stay fresh. Also explore opportunities for physician interviews on Jefferson Exchange, their local talk show.
Continue *Southern Oregon Magazine* advertising.	Recommend re-evaluating and tweaking the ads. Also should explore the opportunity to provide a health article or column with them. Something on common active/sports injuries could be a good fit.
Outreach to Business Community/Employers	
Continue membership in the Chamber of Medford/ Jackson County.	Need to designate someone at the practice to become personally involved and attend Chamber functions.
Community	
Continue participating in Providence Physician Forums.	Currently Dr. Denard and Dr. Kranenburg do these. Dr. Cabalo is supposed to do some in June and July. Determine if there are other physicians who could/should like Dr. Clevenger or Dr. Bengard. Basically, the hospital provides the space and markets the program. They seem willing to do more.
Continue Britt Festival sponsorship.	Recommend that you review sponsorship to ensure you are maximizing this investment. Need to develop a new ad. Recommend something simple with a compelling headline that salutes the festival and provides overall positioning for the practice (i.e. logo, website) within this community. Don't need to include photos of every single physician. Can list physicians' names if room.

continued

PHASE 2: EXTERNAL COMMUNICATION MARKETING

Strategy	Notes
Advertising	*continued*
Explore opportunities for movie theater advertising.	If done properly, can be a great, cost-effective way to reach families in your target market.
Explore digital advertising opportunities.	Can be more cost effective than traditional TV and radio advertising.
Determine if there are any other community publications where you should advertise to maintain brand leadership.	i.e., *Jacksonville Review*
Community	
Challenge each physician and key staff member to identify one community group or organization to become involved in.	When possible, wear SOO logo polo shirts to meetings or when working in the community at events, etc.
Explore opportunities for your physicians to speak at The Manor.	Are there any opportunities here? Certainly is a good target market.
Explore involvement in Rotary.	Dr. Versteeg indicated he is a member of the Medford Rotary Club. Can be a great way to network in the community and build a practice, but is a weekly time commitment. Since Versteeg is a member, could also explore possibility of some of your physicians speaking at their meetings on popular orthopedic topics (i.e. carpal tunnel, arthritis, etc.). They meet weekly so they are always looking for fresh speakers and topics.
Consider positioning yourselves as speakers/resources on orthopedic topics (i.e., arthritis, carpal tunnel, total joint replacement, common sports injuries, etc.) to other local community organizations (i.e. YMCA, churches/synagogues, senior organizations, etc.).	Could help those physicians who are still building their practices. Would require developing a PowerPoint presentation on a timely topic.
Website/Social Media	
Consider starting a blog that highlights topics of interest to your patients.	Helps to keep your web content fresh and optimizes your search engine performance (SEO). Serves as another way to position your physicians as leaders in the field and keeps your patients and referral sources updated on the latest in orthopedics.
	Could identify a list of possible articles/posts and work ahead so it is not a weekly burden to write. These should all be brief.
Determine if you have someone internally to drive and manage your Facebook page.	Currently it is relatively inactive. Facebook users are an engaged audience, and this could be a great opportunity to maintain connections with current and potential patients, but it requires someone overseeing it and making regular posts (i.e., can share new patient testimonial and physician bio videos, photos from community talks and events, links to timely orthopedic articles, promote upcoming talks or events, etc.)

continued

PHASE 2: EXTERNAL COMMUNICATION MARKETING	
Strategy	**Notes**
Media Opportunities	*continued*
Work with the physicians in the practice to identify potential news stories that can be pitched to local media (publications, TV stations as appropriate.)	Can be new treatments, procedures. Local angle on hot national health news topics. Compelling patient story, photos from participation in a community event, etc.

EXHIBIT 2.2 Physician Associates—Sand Lake Pediatrics Marketing & Public Relations Action Plan

Background

These are experienced pediatricians who have been with Physician Associates and in the Sand Lake office for several years. Their volumes are declining slightly, and they face a few new challenges:

1. Loss of insurance contracts.
2. Their office will be moving into a new building in about 18 months.
3. Increased competition.

Strengths

1. Experienced physicians who have been serving the community for more than 20 years. Both are mothers themselves.
2. Offer extended hours — late hours on Tuesday and Wednesday as well as Saturday hours.
3. Same-day sick care appointments available.
4. "Meet and Greet" visits for newborn patients.
5. Full range of care — stitches, minor casting, circumcisions, asthma, ADD, school and sports physicals, etc.
6. Lab and x-ray right across the street — can provide same-day service.

Weaknesses and Challenges

1. Accessibility of current location — They are not in a neighborhood, and there is a lot of traffic congestion in the area.
2. Lack of visibility of current location — They are tucked way back behind the hospital and not on a highly traveled route.
3. A lot of competition in this market, especially out closer to the neighborhoods

Goals

1. Reinforce and strengthen relationships with both current patients and referral sources.
2. Encourage referrals of friends, family, co-workers, etc., from current patients.
3. Begin to establish relationships and referrals in new office neighborhood

(See strategy and notes on page 26.)

Strategy	Notes
Send handwritten thank-you notes. Aim to send 2-3 per week.	Use Physician Associates note cards.
	Send to referral sources — thank your top referral sources, also thank a new referral source after their first referral. Can be a physician, patient, business/ community contact, etc.
	Can also use the note cards to send a note to a patient/parent for something big/memorable mentioned during the visit (i.e., birthday, graduation, winning an award or sports event, etc.)
	Need to keep HIPAA guidelines in mind if sending to a non-physician referral source; must be generic—can't mention patient name.
	A personal note from you will have a powerful impact. It is not expected and people will talk about it, strengthening relationships and generating positive word-of-mouth advertising for your practice.
Send follow-up thank-you note to all new patients after their first visit (thank them for choosing you, provide contact information for appts., prescription refills, etc.)	Let them know you appreciate them placing their confidence in you to care for their child.
	Can also let them know you welcome referrals of friends and family.
Use the note cards to do a New Year's note card mailing to all current patients for each doc.	Thank them for their loyalty. Let them know you are welcoming new patients, accept patients up to age 18, have Saturday hours and would welcome referrals of friends and family.
	Can pre-print on card for each doc and scan in signature.
Create a magnet to distribute to all patients at check-out, reminding them of same-day sick care and extended evening and Saturday hours.	Include logo, Dr.'s names, hours, address, phone # and web address.
	"We're here for you."
	"Offering same-day sick care appointments!"
Cross market within neighboring Physician Associates offices — consider creating and placing a poster in the lobby of the Family Medicine and OB/GYN offices, featuring both pediatricians and letting folks know they are welcoming new patients.	
Talk to the hospital ER about referring unassigned pediatric patients.	
Develop a bio rack card for each doc.	

continued

Strategy	Notes
	continued
Make "thank you" visits to top OB/GYN referral offices.	Bring a handwritten thank-you note signed by the physicians along with a "goodie" from a local bakery (i.e. new Bundt cake shop.)
	Bring new rack cards.
	Ask if there is anything you can do to make referrals easier. Offer to be a resource.
	If the physicians personally do the visits, need to be sure adequate time is blocked on their schedule.
Explore opportunities to speak to prenatal/parent education classes at the hospital.	Can be a great way to meet new parents at a time when they are needing to choose a pediatrician.
Explore opportunities for both physicians to speak at the YMCA or participate in family events there. Develop a 20-minute talk each physician can give. Can also pursue opportunities with other community groups (i.e. mom's groups, family events, parent groups at schools, etc.) if desired.	Ideas: ◦ The Role Sleep Plays in a Healthy Child; ◦ Proper Nutrition for Fueling Healthy Kids; ◦ Five Health Tips for a Happy, Healthy Child; ◦ How Your Child's Health can Impact School Performance.
Make "thank you" referral visits to local preschools and private schools that refer patients as well as to any other key non-physician referral sources.	Bring a handwritten thank-you note signed by the physicians along with a "goodie" from a local bakery (i.e. new Bundt cake shop.)
	Bring new rack cards.
	Also explore opportunities to provide health education to their families. Could you provide any sort of educational forums/talks for their staff and/or parents (especially for back to school?)
Contact nearby elementary schools to see how you could become a community partner/resource. Can you join the PTA as a business partner? Do they have any annual events that you could participate in (i.e. running club, family festival, etc.) Would they be interested in having you speak to their staff/parents?	Let them know you've been serving the community for many years and wanted to reach out to see how/if you could become a resource for them.

50 MARKETING TIPS FOR HEALTHCARE PROVIDERS

As you get started on a marketing plan for your practice, here are a series of useful tips and ideas to help alleviate your concerns about jumping into this new endeavor. You may find some or all appropriate for your practice. As you study these tips, think about how they encompass **The Four A's**. These elements play an integral role in any plan that meets the needs of both your practice and your target groups.

MARKET RESEARCH

1. Start by determining your target audiences. Find out what they want and how they perceive your practice. Begin with your patient satisfaction survey data and then supplement it. You can find a lot online. Gather information from your local Chamber of Commerce, Census Bureau, hospital, the Economic Development Commission in your area, or local university or college, along with other sources.

2. Also consider interviewing a few of your referral sources to find out what they like/dislike about working with your practice. Be sure to include top referral sources as well as any who have decreased referrals.

3. Know your competition, how they are expanding, who they are hiring, and what they're doing. Check out their websites, printed materials and any community advertising they run to see the messages they are sending out.

STRATEGIC PLANNING

4. Begin with a well-thought-out strategic marketing plan that's designed to create awareness, project a positive image, and build and sustain your patient base.

5. Build in a tracking system to measure your progress against your plan. Make sure you understand the reasons for any deviation.

6. Determine the most important marketing project and implement it with appropriate resources. As your practice grows, map out when you can begin the next project. Keep moving your marketing projects forward so that at the end of a year, you can review how far you've come and what should be repeated or deleted from your plan.

IN-OFFICE MARKETING

7. Make your reception area a pleasant, informative place for your patients. Remove the frosted glass left over from the 1980s.

8. Be sure your staff greets each patient by name within 20 seconds of his or her arrival—and with a smile.

9. In addition to the usual and current magazines, stock some on healthcare topics and areas that may be of interest to your patients, such as golf, tennis, travel, fishing, cycling, and autos.

10. Think of creative ways to keep children in your waiting area happy beyond just a TV (i.e., simple toys that can easily be sanitized). Be sure to include children's books and magazines on your shelves. Give children a small puzzle or coloring book imprinted with your practice name to take with them.

11. Keep patients informed on the status of their appointment if you know they're going to be delayed. Learn to apologize and problem-solve with your patients if your office is running behind schedule. Offer patients a chance to reschedule in a timely manner. Remember the **Four A's—Access, Availability, Accountability, and Accommodation.**

PATIENT COMMUNICATION

12. Ensure your website represents your practice in a patient-useful manner. Update it frequently, especially when you open a new office, add physicians or physician extenders, or when you add or change office hours. Enhance **Access** and **Accommodate** your patients by providing a patient portal where they can access lab and test results, complete forms, schedule appointments, etc., at a time that is convenient for them. Create links to interesting, timely and informative healthcare articles, or specific procedures or treatments related to your practice. Or start a blog where you highlight some of the latest health headlines and news developments in your specialty. Add personalized video bios of your physicians to help bring them to life and/or video patient testimonials to help others see and share the patient experience.

13. Develop a professional-looking stationery package that includes logo, letterhead, envelope, business cards, appointment cards, note card and

envelopes, mailing labels, and referral pads and folders, if appropriate for patient handouts.

14. Create patient information sheets for common conditions treated or procedures performed in your office. Make these simple, clean and easy to reference and use. Create a template that complements the design of your stationary package so all of these handouts look consistent and reinforce your branding.

15. Provide patients with a printed summary of their visit, including diagnosis, any new medications (highlighting dosage), referrals or specific instructions.

16. Regularly review all of your online and printed materials, including forms, to assure accuracy and consistency.

17. After a patient's first visit, send a follow-up thank-you letter welcoming them to the practice, expressing appreciation for choosing you, and familiarizing them with any general practice information/procedures (i.e., requesting prescription refills, medical questions, etc.)

18. Have personalized business cards printed for all your staff. Encourage them to use these cards with patients and everyone else they come in contact with. When possible, include a direct phone number (cell phone or land line) so that they can easily be reached.

19. Listen to what your patients ask you. Establish eye contact with them and use their names to show your concern for them.

CUSTOMER SERVICE

20. Remember that it costs 10 times the effort to acquire a new patient than it does to keep an existing one.

21. Be concerned that 91 percent of unhappy patients will never visit again, but that they will make their dissatisfaction known to at least nine other people. That means if you turn off one patient, you discourage 10!

22. Provide personal attention – greet patients by name, track, remember and then ask them about something (i.e., a hobby, grandchildren, etc.) that they shared at a previous visit.

23. Call patients the day after they've had surgery or an office procedure to see how they're doing. You'll be surprised at the positive impact this has on patients.

24. Monitor and evaluate your patient satisfaction survey reports. Look for trends and issues and take action to address any weaknesses or problems.

25. Make it convenient for patients to see you. Evaluate whether you should set practice hours for select evenings, one lunch period per month, and one or two Saturdays per month to accommodate people who can't get to your office during normal weekday hours.

26. Personally give all patients your business card. Thank them for choosing you for their care.

27. Have your staff acknowledge all callers and wait for a response before putting patients on hold.

28. Ask patients if they understand their diagnosis and instructions. Listen to what they tell you.

REFERRAL PHYSICIANS

29. Make referrers feel as if they are part of the team—report to them promptly and send their patients back to them.

30. Send a thorough response—a detailed, diagnostic report—for every referral. If you are doing this through your EHR, make sure the report includes all of the information you would want/need if you were in the referring physician's shoes. If the current EHR template doesn't, work with your EHR vendor to customize it to meet your needs.

31. Be available to referring doctors. Set aside a specific time to return calls.

32. Schedule referred patients as quickly as possible. Set aside a block of time each day for this purpose—and let referrers know about it.

33. Make sure regular referrers know that they are important to you. Stay in touch and thank them regularly with a handwritten note or small gift, or invite them to a special event.

34. Thank the staff of referrers by doing something special for one office each month. Send an appropriate, memorable token of appreciation to the office or have your staff take their staff to lunch.

INTERNAL RELATIONS

35. Review all staff policies and procedures regularly.

36. "Recharge batteries" with staff retreats.

37. Make sure you or your office manager belong to a national professional organization and encourage him or her to keep up to date and attend their meetings.

38. Reward long-time employees with incentives. Find something that is meaningful to them (could be a gift certificate to their favorite restaurant or spa, a paid day off, tickets to an upcoming event, etc.)

39. Hire the right staff. Research and use some of the assessment tools available to help you hire the correct person for specific job responsibilities.

40. Have written job descriptions, hold meaningful staff meetings, and create an employee handbook.

41. Teach your staff to answer the phone and e-mails cheerfully and professionally. Write a script that everyone can follow. Also make sure your staff returns patient phone calls and e-mails in a prompt, cheerful manner; don't ever make a patient feel like a nuisance.

42. Take time to celebrate a milestone or success with your team.

43. Empower your staff to make decisions and keep them proactively informed about any practice changes. (Be sure to set up the necessary systems.)

Community Relations

44. Build time into your schedule to integrate yourself and your practice into the community.

45. Sponsor a community league or team.

46. Contact your local, state, and national government representatives and ask them to keep you up to date on any legislation that might affect your practice. Communicate with them about issues that affect healthcare delivery.

47. Check with employers near your office. Volunteer to contribute healthcare articles, speak at "lunch 'n' learn" sessions, or assist with employee wellness initiatives and events.

48. Make friends with the media.

SOCIAL MEDIA

49. If you decide to incorporate social media into marketing your practice, remember these three key steps: commit, invite and engage.

50. Consider developing a simple "Rate Us Online" card to hand out to patients at the end of their visit. List the web addresses for the key physician rating sites. Also, to ensure **Accountability**, include the name and contact information for a senior-level member of your team in case someone is not satisfied with their experience and wants to discuss an issue.

CHAPTER 3

Developing Bulletproof Referral Relationships

As practice leader, one of your roles is to encourage physicians in your group to develop positive relationships with referring physicians and help develop comfortable ways to enhance those relationships.

You and your physicians will have many different levels of relations with referring physicians. Many of these relationships may have changed as a result of the move to outpatient medicine and the loss of the camaraderie that developed when physicians saw each other daily on hospital floors, in physician dining rooms and at hospital meetings.

But in today's technologically sophisticated reality, it's vital that your physicians focus on these relationships. The question is: Can certain behaviors move those referral relationships along? Definitely!

It sounds very basic, but it's important to note that these referrals often are based on personal relationships. That's why I've asked my friend and colleague, Bob Kodzis, to share his wisdom about the power of great relationships. A nationally acclaimed writer, marketer, and president of Flight of Ideas, Bob also contributed to my previous books.

I believe we can all benefit from his relationship theories, not just for developing relationships with referrers, but also with patients, staff, vendors and others in your world. The following are his insights and specific suggestions focused toward building referral relationships.

BOB KODZIS:
THE POWER OF GREAT RELATIONSHIPS

If I've learned anything during my 32 years in healthcare marketing, it is this: There is no marketing tool or promotion known to man that is more powerful than a good, sincere, and mutually beneficial relationship.

That's a bold statement. And it may be the most important wisdom offered in this book or any other marketing book. The prize of long-term success will go to the practice manager who can find a way to build great relationships with patients, employees, doctors, referral sources and even vendors.

Before we explore the full range of relationships that can propel your business to greater heights, let's talk about what makes a relationship great.

WHAT IS A GREAT RELATIONSHIP?

There are several common traits to all truly great relationships. These traits hold true for personal relationships and professional relationships alike. In fact, I often encourage my clients, when they are unsure how to proceed with a customer or other business relationship, to imagine their business relationships as personal relationships. Personal relationships are much more familiar to us as human beings. And, aside from intimacy and physical contact, the basic premises of personal and business relationships are identical.

1. **One on One**—The strongest relationships we experience as human beings are one-to-one relationships. In their groundbreaking book *The One to One Future*, Don Peppers and Martha Rogers make an extraordinary case for bringing all customer relationships to a one-on-one level. Group relationships are an illusion. If the relationship is not person to person, it's not a real relationship. Businesses do not have relationships with businesses. Patients do not have relationships with your practice. Each patient has a relationship with someone in your practice, and more likely they have a series of relationships with several individuals in your office. One on one is the only way to go when working to build great relationships.

2. **Mutually Beneficial**—Mutual benefit is a critical element of any long-term relationship. Both parties must achieve a significant benefit from the relationship. These benefits do not need to be equal or even similar, but the perceived benefit derived by each side must outweigh the challenges associated with maintaining the relationship. Try this: Do a

"practice relationship audit" on all of your critical relationships to assess which relationships are of greatest value and which relationships are at greatest risk. Relationships that fall on both lists are key priorities for your practice. An example of a practice relationship audit worksheet can be found in Exhibit 3.1.

3. **Altruistic**—In great relationships, participants care about each other beyond the transaction. They look well beyond the question of "What's in it for me?" If you do not truly care about the other person and are not willing to help them beyond the boundaries of your own benefit, you are not in a great relationship. Consider your existing relationships and ask the basic questions "What's in it for them?" and "What can I do to increase the value that they get from this relationship?"

4. **Communicative**—One of the cornerstones of every great relationship is communication. This involves the sharing of information, listening to the information shared, and using that information to further strengthen bonds. A former boss and mentor of mine once gave every member of my marketing staff a framed document to hang over the doors of our offices. It bore four very profound words: "Who needs to know?" It was a spark that helped to ensure that we kept people informed whenever we had information that could benefit or otherwise impact their lives. This handy reminder brought value to all of our professional relationships.

5. **Based in Trust**—It's been said that the greatest evidence of love is trust. The same can be said for a great relationship. Trust is a vital ingredient in any relationship. Building trust takes time, respect, consistency, honesty, integrity and constant communication. In most cases, it must be earned, but once earned, it will clear the path for unlimited growth in the relationship. Different people have different thresholds and requirements before they will extend trust to another human being, but I've found that the best way to build trust is to be trustworthy and to be willing to invest trust before it is earned. There are, of course, risks to extending trust before it is earned, but in my experience, most people step up and perform to our expectations of trustworthiness.

Exhibit 3.1 Practice Relationship Audit Worksheet

Key Relationship	Value we Bring	Value we Get	Risk to Relationship	Possible Solutions
1.				
2.				
3.				
4.				
5.				
6.				

6. **Frequent Personal Contact**—Great relationships require regular, relevant and useful contact. Regularity allows for relationships to progress without feeling as though we are starting all over again. Our relationships, like our bodies, grow rusty if we don't exercise those muscles enough. Relevance is a vital ingredient to regular contact. The purpose

for the contact must be mutually relevant, or we risk leaving one of the participants questioning why we are connecting at all. Finally, the contact must include the sharing of value. Time is our most valuable commodity. If we are going to ask a significant amount of time from each other, we must justify it by ensuring that the contact is relevant and offers value to all. These are investments in the relationship. The care and nurturing of a solid relationship is much like the care of a houseplant. Both require consistency, frequent attention and a watchful eye. Pay attention. Sometimes specific action needs to be taken to allow for growth (pruning.) And beware. If you ignore your relationship for a significant amount of time, it will grow weak and sparse. Neglect it for too long, and it will die.

7. **Great Relationships Are Survivors**—One of the amazing benefits of great relationships is that they are strong enough to survive short-term mistakes, lapses in service, and inconveniences. Weak or nonexistent relationships die the minute things go awry, sending your customers scurrying to find alternate sources to meet their needs. In great relationships, participants are much more willing to give each other the benefit of the doubt and to forgive mistakes.

8. **Willingness to Change**—People involved in great relationships are willing to change and to customize their approach in order to benefit the other people involved. They do so with an understanding that change is sometimes required to ensure the balance of the mutual benefit in the relationship. A relationship with a static person is like dancing around a maypole, and it will grow old very soon. A relationship with someone who is willing to change is more like dancing with a responsive partner and has endless possibilities.

9. **Lifetime Value of a Customer**—This is a principle that was shared with me by a very smart man named George Maynard III. George was the president of a multimillion dollar healthcare foundation associated with an enormous health system where I spent many years learning the intricacies of healthcare marketing. Early in my career, Maynard often played the role of Yoda to my Luke Skywalker. During one mentoring session, he offered these words of wisdom: "I'm not interested in 'hit and run' relationships with our hospitals' donors. I'm interested in the value that they can bring to our organization over the course of their entire lives. I'm interested in the long haul, and I'm willing to do what it takes to foster those long-term (lifetime) relationships." George's words ignited

a thousand-watt light bulb in my head. This principle was not restricted to philanthropy—it applied to every important relationship our business had. During the decades that followed, I have had the opportunity to prove the extraordinary value of this "Lifetime Value" idea again and again. If you or your doctors take the short view on relationships with your key stakeholders, the effort needed to foster long-term relationships may seem to outweigh the benefits of making that effort. Before you reject the lifetime value approach to relationship development, consider these basic facts:

- It costs ten times more to initiate new customer relationships than it does to build upon existing relationships.

- Shallow customer relationships are more susceptible to the advances of your competitors.

- Weak relationships will crumble when mistakes are made or expectations are not met.

People with whom you have strong relationships may eventually act as willing marketing advocates for you and your business at no cost to your practice. In the long term, they inspire economies of promotion, allowing you to spend less on every new unit of business generated. Those who take the short view on relationships are destined to reinvent the marketing wheel every time they enter the marketplace and their overall marketing costs will increase because that is what marketing, printing and media costs do over time … they rise.

NAVIGATING THE WIDE SPECTRUM OF RELATIONSHIPS

While working as the chief marketing officer for a large not-for-profit hospital corporation in Florida, I developed a business model called The Relationship Continuum™ based on some research done by National Research Corporation (NRC) and several years in the field. This model is presented in Exhibit 3.2. My goal in creating this model was to explain to the executives and the board of the corporation, the amount of time, the level of commitment and the investment needed to build long-term relationships with stakeholders in the market; people who had the power to make or break our business.

The basic tenets of this model are simple.

- Relationships take time and attention.

- Relationships only grow stronger if we nurture them properly. This includes, time, attention, responsiveness, and the constant sharing of value and information.

- The key to business success is building relationships with the right people and guiding them to a higher (stronger) level of vestment in the relationship.

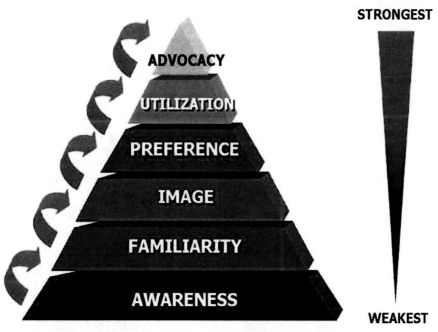

THE RELATIONSHIP CONTINUUM

When I share the Relationship Continuum™ model with my physician clients, my explanation goes something like this:

There are two groups of people in the world: Those who know nothing about your practice and those who know something about your practice.

If we look at the group that knows something about your practice, the largest subset of this group contains those who are AWARE of your practice.

1. **AWARENESS**—Awareness is the "one-night stand" of relationship development. At this level they know something about what you do but not enough to have a well-formulated opinion about the way you do business or your approach to patient care. The most we can hope for at this level is interest in learning more. Those who choose to learn more (and are afforded the opportunity to learn more about your practice and your doctors) will climb to the FAMILIARITY level of the relationship.

2. **FAMILIARITY**—These brave and curious souls will develop a stronger understanding of your practice, perhaps by visiting your website or by talking to some of your patients. They will begin to get a greater sense of who you are and how you do what you do. Because not everyone who is aware of your practice will seek to learn more, the number of people who elevate to the FAMILIARITY level is smaller than the number of people in the AWARENESS level. This is a natural human dynamic. Consider all of the relationships in our lives. We have far more acquaintances than we do people we adore. The Relationship Continuum™ is no different. As the strength of the relationships get stronger, the number of relationships decreases. It's a worthy tradeoff when you consider the lifetime value of the people you serve. Your longest and strongest customers are far less likely to leave your practice because of changes in the market, the advances of your competitors, or a bad experience in your office. They are also far more likely to demand that your practice and your doctors be included in health plans that they are considering for their families. This "pulling" power is priceless in today's seemingly random and fickle healthcare marketplace.

3. **IMAGE**—Some of those who are familiar with your practice will choose to do some more significant exploration and grow to understand the overall IMAGE of your practice. They will know information about your doctors, the plans in which you participate, your locations and perhaps what you do better than any other practice in your specialty. This is one of the most exciting stages in relationship development because we are approaching a decision point. It is also one of the most vulnerable points in relationship development because in many cases, the customer is also exploring your competitors with a similar level of interest. It's a moment of truth … an inflection point. How the employees of your practice respond to customers at this point in the relationship will determine whether or not they prefer your practice over that of one of your competitors.

4. **PREFERENCE**—If you share the right information, at the right time, in the right places, some of those who understand the IMAGE of your practice will develop a PREFERENCE for your practice. They will be willing to give you a try. This is the highest point to which marketing promotions and advertising tools can take your relationship. From this point forward, the strength of your relationship will depend entirely on the quality of care and level of customer service that you provide. Once they develop a preference for your practice, the next logical step in the relationship is UTILIZATION.

5. **UTILIZATION**—When a customer takes the step to make an appointment with your practice, they are taking the ultimate leap of faith. This is a make-or-break moment for your practice. The actions of your doctors and your staff will determine whether they will laud or regret that decision. Everything else up to this point has been a promise. At this tender point in the relationship, the patient will learn whether or not you keep your promises. If you fail to serve them to the level of expectation promised by your marketing and promotions, they will exit this relationship spectrum because their trust has been broken. If this happens, it is extremely difficult and often expensive to win them back. This negative moment of truth becomes even more important when we consider how prevalent and influential customer service review sites have become in recent years. websites like Yelp, Healthgrades, Rate MDs, Vitals and Zocdoc are flooded every day with passionate consumer reviews aimed at healthcare providers. Healthcare is personal so it inspires stronger responses than other forms of service. This is why so many people take to the internet to air their grievances or sing the praises of extraordinary providers and staffs. Potential patients are looking to these review sites for guidance before making healthcare decisions; so are many potential referral sources. **One fact has been proven time and again: patients considering your practice trust patients who have tried your practice.** This means that even one bad review has the potential to inspire many people to steer clear of your practice. Several bad reviews could significantly stem the tide of new patients. It's all about fulfilling your promises at this very fragile stage in the relationship. But don't let the fragility dissuade you from taking bold action. This stage in the relationship is also the one with the most potential and opportunity. If during that moment of truth you not only meet but exceed their expectations, your relationship will progress to the next level and they will become ADVOCATES for your practice.

6. **ADVOCACY**—This is exactly where we want our most important relationships to reside. Advocates are voluntary agents of your practice. They cannot help but promote your business because they have been served so well that they gush about their experience. These are the patients and referrers who are actively saying good things about your practice in person, via social media and on the consumer review sites. Nothing we can say about ourselves in any medium can match the sincere testimonial of a good advocate. A good advocate can also leverage their important and relevant relationships to bring more business to your practice. An avid advocate is worth their weight in gold.

A Two-Way Street

Although much of the explanation of the Relationship Continuum™ model seemed to suggest customers climbing their way to stronger relationships with your practice, nothing could be further from the truth. In most cases, customers won't get on the spectrum or progress to the next relationship level without specific and targeted action by you and members of your practice. The responsibility for building and coddling these relationships rests squarely on your shoulders and the shoulders of your doctors and other team members.

Your goal is to make the whole process and any resulting progressions easy. As the customer is gathering information about your practice, you should also be gathering information about the customer—information that can prescribe the path to a stronger relationship. So ask yourself: What information do I need to be able to serve this customer better than any other practice in town? Then find ways to gather that information in as unimposing a manner as possible. Start with questions like, "How did you learn about this practice?" and "What things are most important to you when you are trying to select a physician?" Continue with questions like, "Can I offer you any information about our practice?" and "Would you like to come for a tour of our office, see our environment and meet some of the staff?"

Proactively Choose Your Targets

Great practices are not created by fostering strong relationships with anyone who shows up at the door. Great practices are built by those who systematically target and make connections with stakeholders who can bring the greatest value to the practice.

Proactively select the kind and quality of people you want to fill and surround your practice. This includes customers, employees, vendors and future associates and partners. You cannot control every aspect of every relationship in your practice, but with diligent attention and persistence, you can steer your business to a much brighter future.

THE VALUE OF RELATIONSHIPS BEYOND YOUR CUSTOMERS

The Relationship Continuum™ was described in terms of your customers, but its power and value do not end with your customers. The quality and depth of all of your relationships have the power to drive every aspect of your business.

Great relationships with your physicians can result in easier compliance with challenges like dictation and documentation. It will also result in a greater willingness to consider your ideas as you work together to grow and refine the practice.

Strong relationships with your employees will increase their willingness to go over and above the call of duty. It will reduce the tardiness, absence and the waste of practice resources. It will enhance employee retention and increase productivity.

Great relationships with vendors can bring extraordinary resources and opportunities to your practice—from additional free samples, to free food and incentives for staff, to inclusion in beta site studies and new product trials.

Strong relationships with referral sources can mean the difference between a struggling practice and a burgeoning one.

There is no marketing tool or promotion that is more powerful than a great relationship. Take the time to evaluate and take greater stock in your key relationships. The return on your investment of time and attention will be healthy growth, meaningful interactions, and the long-term success of your practice.

The Power of Social Media to Enhance Relationships

Many medical and surgical practices include social media as a part of the marketing mix. And most greatly underutilize this powerful tool, often using it as a static medium or an online brochure. The potential for social media is so much greater.

As the most interactive media available, it's a perfect tool to help develop and enhance relationships. It offers assets that many other forms of media do not:

- It allows a laser focus when targeting key stakeholders.

- It is very measurable, and therefore accountable, allowing for real-time assessment of return on investment (ROI).

- It is an amazingly responsive and agile tool, allowing one to shift messaging and focus based on feedback from the target audience. Social media allows for segmentation and sub-segmentation of audiences, resulting in customized information and value provided to each group.

- Social media permeates the boundaries that keep out other forms of media. It goes inside billions of households and millions of businesses because users want to participate. The audience is willing, sometimes eager to interact.

The following are a few recommendations that will help your practice use this powerful medium to better leverage your relationships:

1. **Interact and Evolve.** Social media is all about relationships. That means it will require constant and consistent attention and interaction. A long period of silence or static contribution, and your audience will wander off and choose other places of interest to surf and explore. Without your active interest and engagement, your business will be soon forgotten, so keep it interesting, and keep it going. Find new things to share, new ideas to express. Seek new ways to show your audience how your practice cares about their needs and brings value to their lives.

2. **Bring Value.** Most customers and referrers are tuned into the radio frequency WII-FM - that's "What's In It For Me?" Your response must demonstrate real value. The best social media users provide value to their audiences in the form of information, education, connection to resources, and storytelling. Many appear almost altruistic in their approach to sharing, treating each post like a gift to their audiences. And they are rewarded with multiple visits, robust interaction, message sharing, a healthy internet buzz, and great loyalty.

"People often worry about how often or how rarely they should post. The answer is 'How often do you have something worthy of tapping into my attention?' Do it that often."
— Chris Brogan, Author and Social Media Guru

3. **Be Open and Real.** Social media is about real people connecting to real people. To that end, openness and accessibility are critical. Be sure your interactions are genuine and human. There should be no virtual snow-tinted sliding glass window between you and your audience. Let them in.

4. **Pay Attention and Respond.** Social media is not a one-way medium. It's not a monologue; it's a dialogue. Half the challenge is presenting your value. The more important half is paying attention to and responding to the feedback offered by your audience. Failure to listen and respond will result in a similar exodus as you find in going silent or staying static. *The best way to get someone's attention is to give them yours.*

5. **Keep it One on One.** The strongest relationships are one on one. Use your social media in a way that allows you to interact with individuals and not just the blind masses of the internet. This requires us to bump up the individuality of our responses, including using people's names and tagging them in responses to questions, comments and contributions. It may seem like a daunting task to respond so individually, but the reward is loyalty, support, and even advocacy from your social media allies.

6. **Go Easy on Self Promotion.** So many users of social media focus on self-promotion. To them, it's all about shining the spotlight on themselves in search of the next transaction. This approach to interactive media grows stale very fast and attracts few long-term relationships. Instead, put the focus on the audience. What is most important to them? What do they want and need? What can you offer that intersects with those areas of interest?

7. **Take it Beyond the Medium.** As valuable a tool as social media can be to help develop and evolve relationships, it is not the core of any real, long-standing relationship. It's icing on the relationship cake, not the cake itself. To develop the strongest relationships, you must take your relationships beyond this medium to actual face-to-face connections and

interactions. To get the full value from your social media presence, some or all of your audience need to find their way to your practice, whether as patients, referrers, vendors, or employees; the goal being to shift the relationship from virtual reality to actual reality.

FOSTERING POSITIVE REFERRAL RELATIONSHIPS

Now that you understand the value of relationships in general, thanks to Bob, let's talk about some specific behaviors that can foster positive referral relationships.

Studies show that physicians expect communication about the patients they refer to you, but they also want to know you appreciate their referral. Communicating helps to strengthen and sustain your group's professional relationships. This is enhanced when you develop and implement a plan to keep in touch with them. Here are some guidelines to follow:

1. **Be real.** We live in an electronic age. More and more, one-on-one conversations have been replaced with text messages, e-mails, faxes, EHR reports and social media. While all of this technology has enhanced efficiency, accessibility and accountability, we must be cautious not to sacrifice *quality* of communication for *quantity*. Don't lost sight of the power real relationships with your referring physicians still hold. Reach out. Reconnect. Pick up the phone. Set up a coffee, lunch or dinner date. Then share with each other your challenges, successes, visions and missions. I guarantee it will be time well spent.

2. **Be respectful.** If you find something questionable about a patient's treatment, take it up privately with the referring physician. Unless it's medically necessary, don't repeat tests already performed. This drives up costs and can be offensive to the referring physician as well as the patient.

3. **Make the rounds.** Maybe you are new to your community or perhaps you have brought on an associate or partner who is. How do you get the word out and expand your referral network? Letters and announcement cards are great tools, but almost everyone does them. Very few physicians take the time (which they often have in the beginning) to truly reach out. Put a face with your name. Visit your neighbors and top referring physicians. You can also stop by the hospital and visit the administrative offices, the ER and the Nursing Director. Let them know who you are, what you hope to achieve, and how excited you are to be

a part of their community. Just be sure to make it a two-way conversation. Ask about their needs. Do they have any concerns or new developments you should know about? To make it extra memorable, bring along your business cards and some sort of treat (it can even be healthy), which almost always helps to sweeten the day. We once worked with an OB/GYN who was new to the community, and she took this recommendation to heart, baking and creatively packaging homemade chocolate chip cookies and then delivering them to all of the neighboring offices. And not just to physicians, she also reached out to the nearby hair salon and other local businesses, too.

4. **Drop a note.** Electronic health records have certainly helped to enhance and streamline patient care and communication across providers. Many of these systems even allow you to drop an electronic note to another provider. So are handwritten notes a thing of the past? Absolutely not. While electronic communications are expected, the timeless beauty of a handwritten note card is that it surprises the receiver, and by its very nature shows you went the extra mile. It is unexpected and personal. The delight comes not only in the surprise, but also in knowing someone cared enough to take the time to write something meaningful and sign their name. Make a goal to send five a week. You will do more than make a positive impression, you will make an impact.

5. **Be the welcome wagon.** You may think the welcome wagon too is a thing of the past, but I would argue that like handwritten notes what's old can become new again. We've all been the new kid on the block. It can be intimidating and overwhelming. Develop a plan to contact and welcome new physicians in town. Call or write a personal letter of welcome and introduction. Share with them not only who you are and what your practice has to offer, but more importantly, how you can serve them. You can even go a step further and offer to help connect them to others. Invite them to be your guest at a professional meeting or community event. Enclose your business card, handwrite your cell phone # on it, and encourage them to call if they need anything—even things like recommendations on schools, daycares or other needs of their family. This simple step can speak volumes about your willingness to work together.

6. **Give thanks.** But do it in a different way. Office holiday gifts have become so commonplace that they are hardly even noticed—at least not in a personal way. Why not do something different? For example, you

could give your gift another time of year— Thanksgiving, Valentine's Day or any other time when it isn't expected. Another great way to thank those you work with throughout the year is to "give back" by making a community contribution in their honor. It can be a donation to a local food bank, to an organization that provides healthcare to the homeless, anything that is meaningful to you or those you wish to thank. Many of these local nonprofits are so grateful for your support that they will even mail out personalized cards to those on your list, letting them know that you have made a contribution in their honor. It's unexpected, simple, impactful and even low calorie.

7. **View referred patients as ambassadors.** When patients return to their primary physician and are appreciative of the referral, it helps to build positive relations on your behalf. Be sure to see these patients in a timely manner and communicate appropriately not only with them but with their referring physicians as well.

8. **Notice change.** Make sure you are tracking who is referring patients to you and pull a report each month to monitor this. If you discover that referrals from a certain colleague are declining, call to find out if your practice has done anything to upset or offend them or their patients in any way. Listen carefully to what they say, sincerely thank them for bringing any issues to your attention, promise to investigate further with your staff, and if appropriate, make changes to prevent the issue from arising again. Follow up as necessary to report back on changes or corrections and kindly encourage them to give you another chance.

REFERRAL COMMUNICATION TOOLBOX

Here are a number of different tools and strategies you could incorporate into your referral communication/development efforts:

- Handwritten, personal thank-you notes. Pre-print blank note cards with your logo that you can use for these. (Exhibits 3.3 and 3.4)

- Send periodic brief updates when your group adds locations, providers, services or products.

- Send letters introducing new practice associates and areas of specialization they bring to your practice. (Exhibit 3.5)

- Partner with a referring group to write an informational article or community presentation (Exhibit 3.6). *In Appendix*

- Provide your referral sources with a simple printed piece about your practice that they can provide patients when they refer them to you.

- Develop a referral pad and distribute to referral sources to make the referral process easier.

- Become involved in a key professional group/committee (could be through a professional association, the local hospital, etc.)

- Serve on community advisory boards related to health in your community.

- Write articles for local physician/medical publications. Get to know the editor and suggest timely topics in your field. (Exhibit 3.6) *In Appendix*

- Explore strategic advertising opportunities in local physician/medical publications.

- Investigate sponsorship opportunities at key local community or medical events.

- Encourage each physician in your group to become involved in one community organization or committee.

- Send out announcement cards for new providers joining your practice. (Exhibit 3.7) *In Appendix*

- Create a separate section of your website dedicated to sharing information with your referral sources (i.e. referral information, links to recent medical articles you've published, case studies, etc.)

- Share brief case studies. Showcase in simple, medical terms how you successfully addressed a complex patient problem (could highlight use of a new treatment/procedure, feature a complicated case, etc.) You can print and mail these as well as include them on your website.

- Create white papers on hot topics or advancements in your field. (Exhibit 3.8) *In Appendix*

- Hold an open house or event for referring physicians' staff.

- Partner with a hospital or local university to offer educational programming.

▫ Develop a brochure to educate referring physicians (Exhibit 3.9). *In Appendix* You can have someone on your staff make marketing visits to touch base with current and potential referral sources and use this piece as an educational tool for the discussion and as a leave behind.

EXHIBIT 3.3 Sample Thank-you Note Message to a Patient Who Has Referred to You

Note: You can customize this type of message to suit you as well as to reflect a seasonal or holiday message.

Dear _____,

I just wanted to reach out and personally thank you for your recent referral. I am truly honored and appreciate the confidence you have in our practice. It is patients like you who make my life's work so rewarding. Thanks again and hope to see you soon!

Cordially,

Dr. Smith

EXHIBIT 3.4 Sample Thank-you Note Message to a Physician or Non-Patient Referral Source

Note: You can customize this type of message to suit you as well as to reflect a seasonal or holiday message.

Dear _____,

I just wanted to reach out and personally thank you for your recent referral. I always welcome new patients and appreciate your confidence in our practice. Wishing you good health and hope to see you soon!

Cordially,

Dr. Jones

EXHIBIT 3.5 Sample New Physician Announcement Letter

NAME
PRACTICE NAME
STREET ADDRESS
CITY, STATE ZIP

Dear Dr. NAME:

We are so honored that you continue to trust your patients to our care, and we have some exciting news to share regarding our Fort Worth Office. First, we are pleased to welcome two, experienced retina specialists who have each been serving the Fort Worth community for more than 25 years.

Lee S. Anderson, MD, and **Cliff H. Beasley, Jr., MD**, are joining our practice and will begin seeing patients in our Fort Worth office on November 1. In addition, we are moving to a bigger office to accommodate this growth and better serve our patients. Effective November 9, our Fort Worth office will be conveniently located at:

900 W. Magnolia, Suite 202
Fort Worth, Texas 76104
817-334-0882

A former president and member of the board of trustees of the Tarrant County Medical Society, Dr. Anderson has been in private practice in Fort Worth since 1982 and prior to that, served as chief of ophthalmology services for the USAF Regional Medical Center Clark in the Republic of Philippines. He is an active member of the American Medical Association, the American Academy of Ophthalmology, the Texas Medical Association, and the Society of Heed Fellows in Ophthalmology. Dr. Anderson completed his fellowship in vitreoretinal disease at the University of Miami - Bascom Palmer Eye Institute and served his residency in ophthalmology at the University of Oklahoma Health Science Center in Oklahoma City. He completed his internship in internal medicine at Baylor University Medical Center in Dallas and received his medical degree from the University of Texas Medical School in Galveston.

Dr. Beasley has been in private practice in Fort Worth since 1984 and practiced in Boston prior to that where he also served as a clinical assistant in ophthalmology for Harvard Medical School. In the early 1970s, Dr. Beasley served as a USAF flight surgeon in Little Rock, Arkansas. For the past 20 years, he has also been involved in research as a medical monitor for Alcon Labs. He is a member of the American Academy of Ophthalmology, American Medical Association, Tarrant County Medical Society, Texas Medical Association, Tarrant County Ophthalmological Society, Texas Ophthalmological Association and the Association for Research in Vision and Ophthalmology. Dr. Beasley completed his fellowship in retina and vitreous at Massachusetts Eye and Ear Infirmary in Boston, his residency in ophthalmology at Boston City Hospital, and another residency in family practice at John Peter Smith Hospital in Fort Worth. He served his internship at Parkland Hospital in Dallas and earned his medical degree from Washington University Medical School in St. Louis, Missouri

It remains our honor and privilege to work with you. As always, feel free to call us anytime with your questions, comments or referrals.

Best Regards,

Senior Physician, MD

EXHIBIT 3.10 Strengthening Referral Relationships

Step 1: Build Your Infrastructure

There's a saying that "You don't know what you don't know." You know you need to forge stronger relationships with referring physicians, but where and how to start?

- Develop a monthly report that tracks referrals by source.
- Capture e-mail addresses for both physicians and referral coordinators.
- Create a 90-day trend report.
- Respond immediately to dips.

Step 2: Divide and Conquer

You've built the infrastructure to capture and track referrals. Now it's time to stratify your referring physicians into three groups:

- Top Referrers—These are your most loyal.
- Somewhat Regular Referrers
- Low Referrers—you need to determine here if there are any who should be referring more and create a list of who to target.

Step 3: Develop Your Protocol

You've built your referral tracking infrastructure and stratified your database. Now lay out the expectations for how you and your team will serve your referring physicians:

- Call and/or send a personalized thank you to new referral sources within 24-48 hours.
- Determine patient referral access time.
- Review policies/systems for communicating back to referring physicians.
- Be as service-oriented as possible.
- Commit to report turn-around time.
- Review your discharge communication. Make sure it meets everyone's needs.

This is the tough part. Your team must be consistent—a well-oiled machine. If you make a mistake, own it and communicate proactively.

Step 4: Keep the Fire Burning

From building your database and tracking systems to stratifying your referral base and ensuring you have a service-oriented protocol for handling physician referrals, you're on the right track. Now, you must sustain and build:

- Follow up with your A-list referrers quarterly, and make it memorable. This can be as simple as a phone call, e-mail or personal note. Let them know you recognize and appreciate them. And every so often, when they least expect it, do something special—invite them to lunch or a round of golf, send a personal gift or gift card (something unique and meaningful to them).
- Follow up with your B-list referrers two times a year. They may not rise to the top now, but they still support your practice and with a little nurturing of the relationship, they might rise to become an A-list referrer.
- Call, or better yet, meet with each of the C-list docs you want to increase referrals from. Find out if they have had any issues or concerns with referring to you, promptly address these and get back to them with a solution.

Care Coordination and Careful Communication

Referring physicians have usually spent years developing relationships with their patients. They know they'll be called to help the family sort through issues and complications. For that reason, always engage and partner with the referring physician to plan case management.

If your practice follows a patient for a long time, keep the referring physician informed about the patient's progress. If you find it necessary to refer the patient to another physician, let the primary practice know. Most referring physicians will be annoyed if they're not informed that one of their patients has had surgery or hospitalization. It can be very embarrassing if the patient's family calls the primary doctor and he/she has no idea what is taking place.

Whenever possible and appropriate, remind your physicians and staff to be sensitive and respectful when talking to referred patients—frequently, what your physicians say will be repeated to primary doctors. An off-hand remark or thoughtless statement may come back to haunt your practice.

Some specialists take the attitude that they are fixing a problem the primary care doctor can't solve—that's not conducive to building positive referral relationships. It's better for practice-building if the specialist realizes this and instead, positions for a complementary relationship.

Remember, everyone benefits when referring relationships are open, honest and interactive.

CHAPTER 4

Gaining a Fresh Understanding of Your Patients

Patients are your practice's most important customers. They're the reason you and your group's physicians go to work, continue to update your education, plan for the future, spend your creative and financial resources to upgrade your facilities, and stay compliant with the law. Patients also are one of the primary reasons you must market your services. The **Four A's** are all about how empowered patients have become.

When you think about marketing, you should first concentrate on meeting the needs of your patients or customers. Obviously, their needs can vary from the very simple to the very complex. And though some may require a sophisticated response, most can be met easily—and inexpensively.

BUILDING BETTER CUSTOMER SERVICE

From a functional perspective, patients primarily want to find out if they are ill and, if so, how your practice's physicians or extenders will create a plan to make them better.

From an emotional perspective, patients want to be able to have **Access** to an appointment when it's important to them. They also want both phone and face-to-face exchanges to be unhurried and compassionate, and they want to feel engaged and personally recognized during the time they're connected with your practice.

Here are some basic strategies that can help you foster better customer/ patient service in your practice.

1. **Make customer service a priority.** Confirm everyone you employ knows what service means and how it should be carried out within your practice.

2. **Train your staff to consistently use a patient's or customer's name** no matter how brief the encounter. And if it's an established patient or customer, encourage your staff to remember something about that person and ask about it (could be a job, a child, a hobby, a trip, etc.). Find a way to add these kind of brief notes to the patient record so they can be reviewed and referenced prior to the next visit. Dental offices often excel at this. Your goal is to provide personalized care and make everyone feel his or her needs are important to your practice.

3. **Give customers extra value.** Find ways to recognize long-time patients and referrers for their loyalty to your practice. This can be as simple as a personal handwritten note from the physician.

4. **Information systems and documentation are critical, irrespective of practice size.** By keeping detailed records of patients and referring physicians, you can identify trends that foretell customers' changing needs. And don't just read reports—take action from the information you extract from them. Assign someone to review trend reports and recommend actions for the group.

5. **Use technology wisely.** It's as important as intellectual capital in today's complex world. Patient portals are just one example of how technology can streamline processes for both your patients and staff, enhancing both access and availability. Explore how you can make the most of your system to gather patient input (i.e., patient satisfaction survey) and deliver a higher level of service.

6. **Don't compromise on quality in products, services, or people—especially people.** As in any other industry, creating a valued service experience in healthcare is an exercise in thoughtful details. These experiences support your group's brand name identity and service excellence, which is critical to your success.

7. **Find out what your customers experience at your practice.** Hire a mystery shopper to become your patient, have that person evaluate interactions and experiences, and then have him or her report back to your group, especially on any gaps or opportunities.

8. **Make sure you are employing a patient satisfaction survey tool.** When choosing the company to partner with for your survey, look for those who can benchmark not only your practice, but also your market and specialty.

9. **Track and identify the department/area within your practice that has the most patient complaints each month.** Work with the staff in that area to help come up with solutions.

10. **Reward staff members who openly communicate problems and patient concerns.** Don't criticize. You want them to reveal any mistakes they make rather than hide them for fear of disciplinary action.

11. **Consistently demonstrate your commitment to customer service to your staff, your patients, and others with whom you do business.** Seek anecdotes and opinions from your patients, vendors, and competitors that will allow you to enhance your service. Then, share those stories with your team.

12. **Experience your competitors.** Find out what they offer that could attract patients, payers or employers to do business with them rather than with your practice.

13. **If you have a busy provider, create a waiting list of patients willing to see that doctor on short notice in the event that there is a cancellation.** Ask patients for permission before placing them on the list.

14. **If you don't have one yet, consider offering an online patient portal.** Make sure it is seamlessly integrated and easily accessible from your practice website.

YOUR PATIENT PROMISE

Any successful relationship, especially the doctor-patient relationship is built on a foundation of trust.

What can you promise to your patients that will help to begin to build that trust?

What level of service can you commit to provide that is above and beyond what they have come to expect from a medical office?

Take some time to really think about your "Patient Promise" and put it in writing. Engage your entire team in the process and once established, share it throughout your office and instill it into your office culture. Every single member of your team who interacts with a patient—from registration to patient care to billing—must live and breathe it every day.

Most importantly, deliver on that promise. There is nothing worse than an empty or broken promise. It can do irreparable harm to a relationship. Do what you say you will do. Better yet, occasionally surprise someone by going above and beyond. That is how you make relationships last. And that is the core of successful marketing. Is it easy? No. Is it effective? Absolutely.

Patient Satisfaction

Patients and employees who are selecting and purchasing health plans want to find providers with whom they are familiar. And they want their fears and concerns addressed.

In addition to familiarity and assurance, patients also look for trust and name recognition (brand-name identity). They want to believe that they're with quality doctors who will provide The Four A's. Patients want to believe that their doctors will choose to reduce overhead to become "lean and mean" through business operations rather than by withholding clinical resources.

As I said earlier, some things have changed over time while many others have not. The following list of today's patient preferences reflects the results of numerous focus groups and interviews. It's by no means all-inclusive, but this list will give you a good idea of what most patients want. (Note that many of the items are related to what is of value to the patient who uses the services and the expertise provided by medical practices.)

- Patients want to be able to reach you when they need you.
- Patients want the phone answered by a friendly voice who understands the nature and urgency of their problems.
- Patients want to know how long it will take for someone to return a phone call or e-mail.
- Patients want to have the ability to e-mail questions and get responses promptly rather than wait for phone calls to be returned at the end of the day.
- Patients want to feel valued by all staff, no matter how brief a visit. They do not want to feel like a commodity that simply passes through a doorway with an overhead sign that says "Doctor's Office."
- Patients do not want to believe that every interaction they have with your practice is about money—a deductible, a cost of service, a prepayment before a procedure. If your practice makes a call to welcome a new patient to the practice, that is a "value added" service instead of calls about how a procedure will be financed.
- Patients also want other information, such as:
    - Do you accept their insurance?
    - What should they expect during their visit?

When will they have results of diagnostic tests? If you don't reach them immediately and their test results are problematic, they want to be assured you'll continue to attempt to reach them until you've made a connection.

MEETING PATIENT NEEDS

Satisfying these desires is simple. Most are just common-sense measures that can be implemented by almost any practice in the United States—no matter how large or small. It is the minimum you can do to meet the needs of those with whom you do business. Think of this as a review chart—an exercise checklist to be included in your practice assessment.

- Be sure your reception area is a pleasant, tidy area for patients.

- If you know your practice sometimes runs late and patients back up, provide coffee or fruit juice for patients and visitors in your reception area.

- Update magazines in your reception area so they are no more than 90 days old. Remove old issues and donate them to school libraries. Purchase a subscription to the daily newspaper if your community has one and provide it for patients to read. While many now read it online, there are others, especially older patients, who still prefer a hard copy.

- Create a display in the reception area that highlights your physicians with photos and specialty descriptions. Patients enjoy knowing what their physician looks like before their first meeting.

- Develop a one-page fact sheet that describes your physicians and other providers, your subspecialties, and the services available within your group.

- Have one-page articles available to provide health education. This may include seasonal information and facts about procedures or screenings available within your practice.

- At least once a month, sit in your reception area. Use this time to read the magazines available for patients, look at the décor, and notice what it's like to be a patient in your practice. Change those things that don't make you feel good.

- Invest in some coloring books and other child-safe toys to keep children and parents happy while they're waiting to be seen.

- Make it your goal to have no patient wait longer than 15 minutes during an appointment. Encourage patients to notify your staff if the wait is longer.

OTHER WAYS TO MEET PATIENT NEEDS

Quite often, patient needs are the driving force behind healthcare evolution, as they should be. This phenomenon led to the opening of primary healthcare centers in grocery stores and drugstores. And it happened because patients could not get **Access** to their regular physicians in a time they felt was reasonable. An opportunity was created to meet patient needs, and it's really become quite sophisticated. As with some of the other opportunities that have evolved to compete with group practices, the driving force were **The Four A's.** Patients wanted better **Access, Availability, Accountability, and Accommodation.**

This particular retail medicine concept was created 16 years ago, because a parent named Rick Krieger took his sick son to an urgent care center and had to wait two hours to get a test for strep throat. Mr. Krieger decided there had to be a quicker and more convenient way to get care.

A year later, he and his new partners—one of whom was a physician—founded QuickMedx, the retail healthcare clinics that became MinuteClinic. Their first healthcare centers opened in Minneapolis in Cub Foods stores. They focused on seven common acute medical conditions that patients often suffer from: strep throat, mono, bladder infections, ear infections, sinus infections, pregnancy testing, and the flu. Now, MinuteClinic has healthcare centers in several CVS Pharmacies throughout the country.[1]

The situation is really quite simple. Your patients want to see you on what they consider to be a reasonable time schedule. If they, their child, or their spouse is ill, they want to be seen by a physician or a healthcare extender who can prescribe medication or treat their problem.

Patients are no longer necessarily loyal to their personal physician practices. If you don't meet their needs—if they can't be seen when they want to be seen—they'll look for another way to be accommodated. And it's often right at their fingertips.

In many communities, they can go to their neighborhood pharmacy and be seen quickly. They can enter their cell phone number and request a text message alerting them when the provider will be ready to see them so they can go and shop or run errands while they wait. And that's an important benefit for today's busy, overscheduled parents. Then they can move directly from the caregiver to the pharmacy to get a prescription filled and pick up Gatorade, throat lozenges, or whatever else they need to make their life a little more comfortable.

---

1 CVS. MinuteClinic. CVS.com. http://www.cvs.com/minuteclinic/

As you face this and other competition to traditional group practice care, you must be sensitive to the things that are of value to your patients and find creative ways to deliver what they want.

CHAPTER 5

Building Better Customer Service

One of the most important tenets of marketing maintains that you must know your customers. As discussed, healthcare marketing "customers" primarily translate to patients, but they also include your referrers and others, including your staff. And after you know them well, you must try your best to meet their wants and needs, even as your practice evolves. Toward this goal, many practices create mission statements and vision statements, some even define their core values.

No matter what the process, successful practices find a way to address customer service issues because they realize that's the cornerstone of their success. Although some of these issues may not sound important, they are vital to your patients. These issues include the following:

- How long it takes to get an appointment;
- How long callers spend on hold;
- How long it takes to see a physician or extender beyond the time of an appointment;
- How quickly phone calls and e-mails are returned;
- If physicians call back a family caregiver in a timely way;
- Whether parking is readily available;
- Whether signage is friendly and easy to read;
- Whether staff exhibits a patient-friendly attitude.

Even when you try hard to meet customers' needs, the task can seem impossible. How can your practice focus on serving patients when your physicians are focused on practicing medicine? They still have to concentrate on making the right diagnostic and treatment decisions, keep up with changing regulations, and understand and manage overhead costs. All of this while they watch their incomes being compromised and see creative competitors carve away at what once was a stable patient base.

That said, realize that marketing and communications are fundamental factors in the business of medicine, and customer/patient service is the single most important element of any marketing program. First, understand that providing service and managing your brand in the face of cultural, behavioral, and economic shifts is an ongoing, evolutionary process. Then, continually plan for changes that translate into service and accommodation for your customers/patients.

START WITH YOUR STAFF

You may have great physicians who are highly trained in their specialty and hail from some of the finest medical institutions in the country. They may be compassionate and listen. They may be great about educating and involving patients in their care plans. And their patients may absolutely love them.

But do your patients love your staff, too?

Are they greeted warmly and treated with respect and privacy?

Does the nurse or medical assistant who takes them back seem to know them, listen to their concerns and answers to the standard health questions make them feel comfortable and put them at ease?

People make impressions of us based on the company we keep. Make sure your staff is a reflection of the practice you want to have. Here are a few tips:

- **Make a good hire.**
- **Provide adequate and ongoing training.**
- **Set the right leadership example.**
- **Empower your staff to be problem-solvers.**
- **Stop to celebrate.**

This last tip bears emphasizing. Everyone is moving 100 mph these days, powering through our daily to-do lists. As administrators or physician leaders, we are happy when things go well and we achieve goals, yet too often we jump right on to the next project or agenda item. *STOP.* Take a moment to celebrate, to thank, to recognize. Whether it is a major accomplishment, or perhaps more important, someone who is doing the right thing day in and day out, take a moment to thank those on your team. We're often quick to point out problems and opportunities for improvement. We need to be just as vigilant about celebrating successes, even the small ones.

The Power of a Balloon

My colleague's fiercely independent grandmother fell and broke her hip on her 94th birthday. A day that was supposed to be spent celebrating with family was instead spent, frightened and in agony, in the ER. Although in great pain, she kept her sense of humor and quickly developed an attachment to her ER nurse. The nurse shared how she was headed out of town for a college football game as soon as her shift was over. When the nurse asked if there was anything else she could get my friend's grandmother, the elderly woman quipped, "a birthday balloon sure would be nice."

The story could have ended here, but it didn't. My friend's grandmother was later moved up to an inpatient room to prepare for hip surgery the next day. An hour after she was settled in her room, there was a knock on the door. In walked the ER nurse holding a Happy Birthday balloon. Even though she was "off duty" and in a hurry to get out of town, she made the time to get a balloon and deliver it to a patient who was no longer on her watch. And it didn't end there. Two days later, that same nurse, on her lunch break, visited the elderly woman to check and see how "her patient" was doing after surgery.

This nurse put the "care" in healthcare. She certainly did not have to do all she did. It was not in her job description. She took the initiative. She made the time. She cared. With reimbursements increasingly dependent on patient satisfaction, something as simple as a balloon and a visit went a long way.

YOUR OFFICE ENVIRONMENT

You know the old saying, "if these walls could talk?" Well, they do. And so do your doors, your registration desk, your parking lot and even your bathrooms. What messages do they send? Are they the right ones? Let's take a look at a few examples of how your office environment can shape patient experience and satisfaction.

WHAT DOES PARKING HAVE TO DO WITH MARKETING?

A lot. Other than the phone call to make an appointment and perhaps a visit to your website, it is a patient's first experience with your practice and can shape their first impression. Are you making a good one?

- Is your parking area well marked?
- Are there an ample number of spaces, including handicapped spaces?
- Is there a designated and easy-to-use patient drop-off area?
- Do you have an overflow option for busy days?
- Is all of this clearly communicated to your patients with prominent signage, on your website and by your staff when they schedule patient appointments?

We're all familiar with the old adage of "walking in another's shoes." When was the last time you "drove in your patient's shoes?" Take a test drive on your way into the office tomorrow. Look at everything through their eyes. What needs to change? Do it again at other times of the day.

Parking is a part of the patient experience and as a result, your brand. You can have the best doctors on the planet, but if a patient can't find a place to park, they may be late to their appointment. That means they may already be anxious and maybe angry when they walk through your door. You are already starting off on the wrong foot.

Don't let this happen. Make sure your patient parking is meeting their needs.

THE GLASS WALL

So now your patient has parked, and they are walking in your front door. What happens next?

We've all heard of the glass ceiling but what about the glass wall? It is that barrier to service—sometimes real and sometimes just perceived—when you first walk into a physician's office and no one welcomes you.

Remember the frosted sliding windows (some even had doorbells) that were so common in doctor's offices in the 1970s and 1980s? Sadly, I still encounter them. Not only are they ugly and unfriendly, these physical barriers seem to say: *"Whatever I'm doing is more important than saying 'Hello' to you and making you feel welcome to our practice. It doesn't matter that you may be nervous, scared, confused or just not feeling well; we don't care yet.* " These "windows" are really closed doors. They feel cold, impersonal and institutional.

I have also visited many practices that may not have a physical window yet the barrier is just as real because no one greets patients as they enter. It only takes a moment to smile warmly, make eye contact, welcome someone and spark a connection. Patients have more choices than ever before. As providers, you need to make sure your patients feel welcome from the moment they enter your door.

THE ART OF PRIVACY

So you've passed the parking and welcoming test, what comes next? In a word, privacy.

Thanks to social media, our lives are more public than ever before, yet privacy has become an increasingly valuable and fiercely guarded right and value. For a variety of reasons, many patients would prefer to keep their medical condition(s) private. And while healthcare privacy laws abound, many medical practices still miss key opportunities to meet this need of their patients.

How do your patients "sign in"? Does someone personally greet them and handle the process? Or do they sign in on a sheet with the names of other patients in the waiting room? While a personal touch with immediate care is always best, at the least, have your patients sign in on a label and then immediately remove the label before the next patient signs in.

When it is time to call the patient back to an exam room, does your nurse or medical assistant stand in the doorway and yell out the patient's name?

What if you train your team to discretely coordinate or remember patients and then have them walk up to the patient in the waiting room, confirm their name and personally invite them back. Or if you have a very large, busy practice, why not take a cue from restaurants and issue each patient a pager upon signing in and then page them to the desk when you are ready? These seemingly simple steps demonstrate to your patients that you respect their privacy and value them as individuals.

CAREGIVER OR CASH REGISTER?

In addition to basic customer service and privacy, one of the other common stumbling blocks for many medical practices is billing.

In the face of shrinking reimbursements, healthcare providers are working harder than ever to maximize collections and boost the bottom line. But at what expense? Can you take it too far? Take some time to explore your current processes:

- How do you communicate the cost or patient responsibility for your services?

- When do you communicate these costs? Is it before the appointment or in advance of a procedure so the patient comes in prepared and knowing their responsibility?

- Do you verify insurance coverage prior to the appointment so the patient knows upfront and is not hit with any surprise charges?

- Do you allow adequate time for patients to make payment?

- Do you offer payment plan options, especially for high-cost services?

- How do you communicate your payment policies? Is it in a warm, friendly, personalized way or is it in cold, legal terms on your website or using bold black type on a white piece of paper taped to the waiting room wall?

It is critical to remember that while revenue is important, patient experience and satisfaction carry increasing influence on your reimbursement. If your patients perceive that you are focusing too much or pushing too hard to collect payment, you run the risk of negatively impacting the patient experience.

No doubt you must be fiscally prudent and responsible. Just spend some time evaluating the way you handle and communicate billing, and determine if improvements could be made. At the end of the day, make sure your patients view you first as a caregiver ... not a cash register ... or you risk losing them altogether.

The Waiting Game

Waiting. It is probably one of the top service complaints patients have.

Although there are certainly ways to reduce patient wait times, in healthcare, there will always be times when waiting is inevitable. Do you seize those times as an opportunity? You should.

Too often, we don't. We're busy. We triage. We move onto other patients and issues.

Patients waiting are often anxious, frustrated, worried, nervous, and depending on the situation, maybe even scared.

What can you as the healthcare provider do? It's simple: Communicate.

Stay in contact. Set a time period (every 15 minutes, 30 minutes, etc.), and personally check in with the patient. Acknowledge. Apologize. Reassure. Inform.

Give each patient an update on why there is a delay and how much longer you think it might be. If patients understand what is going on, what to expect and when it might happen, they are much more likely to relax and wait patiently. If it is not an urgent matter, offer the patient an opportunity to reschedule or come back later. If a patient chooses to wait, offer something to drink, encourage him/her to make any phone calls if needed, use the restroom, have a snack, etc.

No one likes to wait, and you should make all efforts to minimize wait times within your office. However, when it can't be helped, by checking in and staying in contact, your patients (and their families) feel valued. They know you have not forgotten them and that you are keeping them at the top of your mind. And that can make all the difference.

Practice What You Preach Or Pay The Price

Today many medical practices charge a fee for cancellations within 24 hours, ask patients to arrive early for their appointments (anywhere from 10-30 minutes) or have a policy and consequences for being late. None of those seem unreasonable unless:

1. You (the physician's office) have to cancel the appointment at the last minute. This happened to a colleague of mine recently after she had already taken time off from work and planned her day around the appointment. Worse yet, when she went to reschedule, they couldn't schedule a new appointment until the following month.

2. The patient arrives early or on time as requested and has to wait well beyond the appointment time (maybe an hour or more)

What happens then?

If not handled correctly, angry patients may go on Facebook or Twitter (often on a smart phone while sitting in your waiting room or an exam room) and vent their frustrations. Soon, what started out as a singular bad experience is now broadcast to the patient's entire social network. Sadly, I see these kinds of posts several times a week.

Perhaps you should re-examine your policies and proactively come up with some positive actions you can take when these types of unforeseen incidents happen. Things like:

1. Establish procedures and timelines for how and how often to communicate with the patient, apologize and keep them updated on a situation.

2. Offer to order them lunch or provide a gift card to a nearby restaurant or coffee shop.

3. Send a personal, handwritten note within 24 hours, apologizing again and assuring them you do everything in your power to avoid such situations.

Most people are remarkably forgiving if they feel someone sincerely apologizes, cares and does something to make amends. However, if they feel taken for granted, they will make sure others know how they were treated. And with social media, this is easier, more far-reaching and more damaging than ever before.

THE BUCK STOPS HERE — THE IMPORTANCE OF ACCOUNTABILITY

One of the most overlooked and underused of the **Four A's—Accountability**—is perhaps one of the best for boosting customer service and building stronger, more authentic patient relationships.

Despite the best laid plans and procedures, things go wrong. We are all human, and none of us is perfect. What can differentiate your practice from others is how you respond when mistakes happen or things don't go according to plan. Do you take responsibility? Do you empower your staff to do the same?

I once called a doctor's office to make an appointment. Something was wrong with their phone system and rather than connecting me with the appointment desk, it looped me through directly to the billing department—not once but twice. After the second time, the billing representative on the other end of the line apologized profusely and stepped in to solve the problem. She took down my name, number and reason for calling, and said she would personally walk over to the appointment desk and make sure someone called me right back. Sure enough, within 10 minutes my phone rang, and a scheduler from that office also apologized and set up my appointment.

Was I frustrated when I initially couldn't get through? Yes. Was I even more frustrated when it looped to the billing dept. the second time? Of course. But then someone stepped in, took responsibility (for something not in her job description), and ultimately solved the problem. And while initially frustrated, I left the experience with a good feeling about this practice, confident that they had my best interest at heart and were accountable for the care I receive.

Are your employees empowered and motivated to do the same?

Don't Play the Technology Blame Game

Technology is revolutionizing the healthcare industry, and it is here to stay. Patient portals and electronic health records (EHR) are becoming the rule. These tools can enhance co-ordination of care as well as **Access, Availability, Accommodation and Accountability.** However, as with any technology, it is only great when it works. And when it doesn't? That is when human care, concern and **Accountability** must kick in. Here is a common scenario I hear all too often from patients:

Patient sees the physician for a routine or follow-up visit.

The physician authorizes refills on a maintenance prescription, and with a click of a but-ton on the EHR, sends it to the patient's pharmacy. Beautiful! Efficient! Technology at its best!

Only, it didn't work …

Patient is headed out of town and runs into the pharmacy to pick up the prescription—but it isn't there. The pharmacy says they never received it. The patient calls the doctor's office and has to leave a voice mail message.

Patient receives a call back, assuring her the practice resent the prescription authorization.

Patient calls the pharmacy—they still haven't received it.

The finger-pointing blame game begins.

He said. She said.

Back and forth, back and forth, for days.

And all the while, the patient is concerned she won't receive the medication in time for her upcoming trip and will and end up with health issues far away from home and her physician.

The loser in this game? The patient. And I would argue the physician's office as well.

Finally, a human who cares steps in. Only it isn't someone in the physician's office; it is a pharmacy tech.

He immediately recognizes and acknowledges the patient's exasperation, apologizes and says he will personally make sure the issue is resolved within the hour. And it is.

How does the patient feel about her Dr.'s office now? How about her pharmacy? How would you feel?

In this age of technology, nothing replaces a compassionate, accountable human being who will accept responsibility and take the initiative to solve a problem. No computer can provide that. Is your team ready to step in and stop the blame game?

BUILDING LOYALTY

The majority of today's "prosumer" patients have plenty of choices when it comes to selecting a physician, and their expectations tend to be high. Yet, in the world of healthcare, much of it is the same. The experience at one medical office differs little from another, and among those experiences, there are certainly too many negative ones. And thanks to the social media world we live in, these negative stories are instantly amplified and broadcast. But standing out from the pack, generating good "buzz" and building a loyal patient base doesn't have to cost a ton of time or resources. It is often the little things that can separate you and get folks talking.

So how do you not only attract new patients, but increase loyalty and build life-long patients?

Dazzle

Healthcare is an experience. Make it an exceptional one. Stand out. Think about what you can do in your practice to not only meet your patient's service expectations, but exceed them. What can you do that is different from others in your community? Something that will be memorable and meaningful to a patient. It could be as simple as a follow-up phone call; a well thought-out, sincere and personal explanation of a condition or concern; or a handwritten thank-you note. Express yourself and let your patients get to know you a bit as a person. Share a story, ask about a patient's hobby or career and spark a conversation, wear a signature accessory (one physician I know always wears bow ties while another pediatric physician likes cartoon and character ties), share and express your personal interests in your office décor by hanging unique artwork or photos (maybe you run marathons, coach a little league team, travel to interesting places, or like to take hikes and shoot nature photography), make the effort to work established patients in immediately when they have an urgent issue. It's often the smallest things that make the biggest and longest lasting impression.

Apologize

When you or someone in your office has done something wrong, make it right. No office is perfect. You get called out to perform an emergency surgery, and a patient is left waiting. Or a schedule blunder occurs. In the world of healthcare, it is inevitable that these things will happen occasionally, even in the best-run practice. Ironically, if you acknowledge the problem immediately, take the time to personally and sincerely apologize, accept accountability, and then go one step further by doing something to "make it right," you may have just strengthened a patient's emotional ties and loyalty to you. It could be as simple as a personal phone call (be sure to listen and not do all the talking); a thoughtful, hand-written note; a gift card to the nearest coffee shop. Just remember what you do isn't necessarily as important as how you do it.

QUANTIFY

Ask your patients about their opinions and experiences. Once again, this helps to build a connection. People want to know their opinions are sought and valued. Closely monitor your patient satisfaction survey report and share the results. And don't be afraid to go one step further. If you have patients who have had exceptional experiences with your practice, ask if they would allow you to share their "stories" with others (i.e., through a patient testimonial video on your website) or encourage them to share it themselves on social media. You can even provide reminder cards at checkout that encourage satisfied patients to visit one or more of the many physician rating websites and share their "review." Give your patients a voice.

COORDINATE

In the increasingly complex and ever-changing maze we call healthcare, many patients just want to know there is one person they can call to help them navigate the system and answer their questions. In many successful practices and medical organizations, this takes the form of a Care Coordinator. To patients, this person becomes their resource—the one person they can count on to be there, to answer their calls and to help coordinate their care—from medical questions to prescriptions to referrals to procedure scheduling to community resources. You've alleviated patients' fear and reduced their stress. You are also well on your way to building a loyal patient. Why would they want to go anywhere else?

REMEMBER

Remember to smile. The power of a smile—whether face to face or over the phone (yes you can "hear" it)—can be just what patients wish would happen but not what they expect.

Your patient is a person. At each visit, jot down something personal or memorable that the patient shares and then ask about it at the next visit. It can make that six-month or annual visit seem so much more personal.

"Mrs. D., how is John liking his first year of college at ABC University?"

"Mr. H., how was that golf clinic you went to? Did it help your short game as you hoped?"

"Mr. B, is your daughter still playing softball? How are those showcase tournaments going?"

"Ms. T., how was the family reunion you were so busy planning the last time I saw you?"

Now you are more than just a doctor, you are someone who cares. And that goes a long way toward building loyalty.

Five Little Things
That Make a Big Difference

Want to improve patient satisfaction? Strengthen referral relationships? Attract and retain patients? Try these on for size.

1. *Smile.* It's that simple if it is sincere.

2. *Compliment.* And make it genuine. Make it your goal to find something special or positive about each person you meet and tell them.

3. *Remember.* Try to remember something about each person you meet and then ask about it next time you see them. And with today's technology, it is easier than ever before to make note of that "something" to help you remember.

4. *Write a personal thank-you note.* It may be "old school," but in our techno world, it is more impactful than ever before.

5. *Be on time.* Better yet, be a few minutes early.

The best things always come in small packages.

Lessons Learned from a Sanitation Worker

You might not think a medical practice has anything to do with garbage collection. Yet, a friend of mine recently shared a story that drew the connection for me.

Debbie has had the same trash collector for at least 15 years. Every Monday and Thursday, he arrives on time with a huge smile on his face and a friendly "Good Morning. How 'ya doing?" If the weather is bad, he even takes the time to move her cans up near the house.

When Debbie's son was young, he loved trucks, and the little boy would wait at the window so he could run out to greet the garbage truck and watch the "action." The sanitation worker would always take the time to talk to him for a couple minutes before moving on to the next house. If the little boy wasn't at the window, the truck would honk and wait an extra minute to give the little boy a chance to come out.

To this day, if Debbie is outside when the truck goes by, the driver always honks and waves even if she is in a different part of the neighborhood picking up the morning carpool. Debbie's son is now almost 10 and rarely home when the garbage truck comes. Still, if Debbie happens to be outside, this sanitation worker will always stop, get out of his truck and take a moment to ask about "how his little buddy is doing—what grade he is in, what sports he is playing, how school is going—" and tells Debbie to tell him "Hello and that he misses seeing him."

Arriving on time. Smiling. Having a great attitude even if your job "stinks." Greeting folks warmly. Remembering. Making the most of each human contact and connection. Taking an extra minute out of your day to have that one-on-one conversation and deliver that extra bit of service. Isn't that what it is all about? How much better would your practice be if everyone took a lesson from this sanitation worker?

ACCESSIBILITY

All of the things we've talked about so far that are key to building better customer service in your practice—your staff, your office environment, accountability and loyalty—all hinge on the last item I would like to cover: **Accessibility**. If people can't get a hold of you when they need you, nothing else matters.

Fortunately, technology has helped to make it easier to provide your patients with increased **Access**. From online scheduling to patient portals, the healthcare industry keeps finding innovative ways to meet the expectations of today's prosumer. I would caution you though that while these technologies can certainly enhance service and should be a part of your toolbox, be careful not to lose the human touch. Here are a couple of examples to illustrate my point.

BROKEN BRANCHES AND DEAD LIMBS—THE PROBLEM WITH PHONE TREES

Phone trees. Almost every business has them yet you rarely meet a customer who likes them. Yes, the efficiency "results" may look good on paper, cutting down on expenses, but at what cost?

Put yourself in your patients' shoes. When was the last time you made a call—whether it be to a physician office or your insurance company—and had a wonderful experience with a phone tree, one that enhanced access and service, and made you feel elated about that company/organization and valued as a customer?

Occasionally, there are phone trees that work. If all I have to do is order a refill on my prescription, I like that I can call up my pharmacy at any time that is convenient for me, punch in the right numbers, and it is ready for me to pick up at my desired time.

However, most of the time when I call a business, especially for medical reasons, my needs are not that simple. And frankly, the computer often fails. I run into broken branches and dead limbs on that phone tree that limit my ability, waste my time, and leave me feeling frustrated and sometimes even angry. Is that how you want your patients to feel about your practice?

In this day of increased demands for value, patient satisfaction and accountability, most phone trees don't cut it. Patients want a human touch. You may be the best physician in your specialty, but if every time I call I can't get a human being and worse yet, have to leave a message that goes unreturned, I will not stay with your practice. And if I am a prospective patient "shopping" for a new doctor, do you think your automated phone answering system will make me feel welcome and want to stay?

There are many aspects of today's healthcare system that are broken. Some are quite complex and difficult to remedy. Having a warm human being answer your phones rather than a cold computer is an easy fix, and I would argue a marketing investment that will pay in spades.

UNRETURNED CALLS: IS ANYONE LISTENING?

In addition to phone trees, one of the most frustrating **Access** service issues patients face is unreturned calls.

Everyone misses calls sometime. It should be minimized even in the busiest of medical practices, but it is inevitable. Like many of the other service issues we have discussed, how you handle missed calls can make all the difference.

A lot of it starts with attitude. When a patient leaves a message, does your staff view it as an opportunity to reconnect and dazzle or just another annoyance in the day, or worse, something to be ignored entirely?

As with any business, unreturned calls are lost opportunities. And lost opportunities can lead to lost customers/patients.

A friend of mine recently had a physician's office call to reschedule her appointment. She was at work in a meeting and missed the call. She called back as soon as she could but had to leave a message. No one returned her call. She waited a day, called back again and had to leave another message. Still no return call.

Another friend called her doctor to request a copy of her medical records because a specialist she was seeing requested them. She, too, had to leave a message. No return phone call. She called again. Still no call back.

Both are now leaving their respective doctors and understandably so. Different doctors. Same ending. And all it would have taken in both cases was a phone call returned in a timely manner by a warm, helpful staff person.

Do You Really Care?

A new, elderly, arthritic patient walks into your office. She hands you the completed new patient paperwork that was sent to her ahead of time. However, a few items are missing—some from her referring physician and some from additional forms you need her to complete. The patient is clearly nervous, rattled and upset because she thinks she has done everything that was needed. Do you hand her a pen, slide the window shut and go about your work? Or do you offer to help her call the referring doctor's office? Do you ask if she needs to use a phone? When you see her arthritic hand fumbling with the pen, do you offer to help her? Do you care?

Another elderly patient walks into your office for a routine diabetes visit. You check her vitals, and her blood pressure is clearly elevated. Do you explain it away as nerves, move on with the exam and send her on her way? Or do you talk to her for a bit, monitor her condition and then check it again to see if it has gone down? Do you offer to call a friend or family member to come be with her? Do you care?

Reimbursement reforms have made patient satisfaction more important than ever. Are you taking advantage of this opportunity?

Every day, you and your team have the opportunity to just do your jobs, or to go a step further—to stand out and really care. Consider the after-hours urgent care physician who takes the time to call all of his patients the next day to see if they are feeling better. Or the pediatrician who notices that in addition to the little boy he is examining, mom or big sister looks or sounds bad and also needs medical attention. Or the orthopedist who takes the time to ask about and listen to his young patient's athletic dreams and training, and works with her on a compromise treatment plan that allows her to heal while still being able to play the game she loves.

Caring is no longer just a choice. It is necessary for survival and success in the medical marketplace. Do you really care?

SUMMARY

Prosumers have high service expectations, and if you can't meet those needs it is easy for the prosumer to find another physician practice that can. Make the time and take the time to do the **Four A's** right—your survival in the current medical marketplace depends on it.

Stay alert to your customers' needs and desires.

Understand the importance of **The Four A's: Access, Availability, Account-ability** and **Accommodation.**

Recruit, motivate, and retain good employees.

Create a warm, welcoming and easily accessible office environment.

Take responsibility when things go wrong and empower your team to do the same.

Develop your own service standards, strategies, and tactics to improve your customers' experiences and strengthen their connection and loyalty to you.

If you truly provide service and manage your brand, you'll have no trouble maintaining your current patient base and growing your practice as you desire.

CHAPTER 6

Diagnosing Your Practice— A Simple Guide to Effective Practice Assessment

It's no secret that the healthcare industry has seen tremendous change in recent years and remains in a state of flux, especially with the implementation of the Patient Protection and Affordable Care Act (ACA). While more Americans are now insured, changes continue to occur and barriers and challenges remain.

- Since the passage of the ACA, about 16.4 million uninsured people have gained health coverage.[1]

- According to a 2015 national survey of primary care providers by the Kaiser Family Foundation/Commonwealth Fund, 59 percent of physicians and 64 percent of nurse practitioners and physician assistants reported that they have seen either an increase in Medicaid patients or patients who were previously uninsured since the ACA coverage expansions took effect.[2]

---

1 U.S. Department of Health and Human Servcices. Healthcare Fact Sheets. http://www.hhs.gov/healthcare/facts-and-features/fact-sheets
2 The Kaiser Family Foundation and The Commonwealth Fund, "Experiences and Attitudes of Primary Care Providers Under the First Year of ACA Coverage Expansion," June 2015

• According to the Kaiser Family Foundation/Commonwealth Fund study, providers feel the amount of time they have with each patient and the time they spend on insurance administration issues have gotten worse.[3]

And then there is the issue of acquisitions and physician employment by large healthcare organizations. While this is a reality for many practices and communities, some in the industry believe this trend is leveling off and may even be reversing due to profitability challenges coupled with a more entrepreneurial approach taken by many private physician practices.[4]

I like to think of it as the old adage of turning a challenge into an opportunity. Is it easy? No. Is it possible? Absolutely.

If your practice is like most and if you want to succeed, things must change. Obviously, you can no longer conduct business as you've done in the past. No successful practice can. And as lead physician or practice administrator with fiscal responsibility, you know this better than anyone.

So what should you do? What can you do?

First, on the operations side, monitor and control your practice's revenue cycle activities, utilize today's technology, and analyze the way you operate. Find new ways to operate efficiently and effectively without compromising customer service.

As a manager, you should look at the roles of both clinical and non-clinical staff to ensure efficiency without compromising care. Find ways to schedule patients more efficiently, which may require you to make big decisions about business hours and overhead. To meet your patients' needs and compete with the proliferation of urgent care centers, you may have to schedule patients early in the morning, late into the evening, or even on weekends.

As you assess your practice, you need to look at how well you respond to the changing needs of your environment—for what is occurring in your community now and for what is coming. But before you begin your assessment, you have to look at the big picture.

One of the key issues is to understand the population around you. Who are they in terms of demographics, such as age, income, profession, health status, and

---

3 The Kaiser Family Foundation and The Commonwealth Fund, "Experiences and Attitudes of Primary Care Providers Under the First Year of ACA Coverage Expansion," June 2015
4 Forbes, "The Private Medical Practice is Not Dead Yet," June 2015.

other defining information? And if you have multiple offices, you have to realize that this demographic may differ from community to community.

According to the Centers for Disease Control, as of 2012, 117 million people—*approximately half of all adults*—had *one or more chronic health conditions*, and about 25 percent had two or more.[5] These chronic diseases, which include heart disease, obesity, stroke, type 2 diabetes, cancer and arthritis, are among the most costly and preventable of all health problems. In fact, in 2010, 86 percent of all healthcare spending was for people with one or more chronic medical conditions. Total costs of stroke and heart disease alone were estimated at $315.4 billion in 2010, while the total estimated cost of diagnosed diabetes in 2012 was $245 billion. Meanwhile, obesity remains a significant health challenge with more than one-third of adults defined as obese in 2009-2010.

Let's face it, the U.S. healthcare system, especially physician practices, is having to cope with not only a rapidly changing marketplace and new regulations, but also the needs of a growing number of individuals, including aging baby boomers, who have increased healthcare issues and high medical costs.

A 2015 physician compensation report by Medscape revealed a few interesting statistics and trends about how physician practices are faring in this new world.[6]

- The $284,000 average compensation for specialists and $195,000 for primary care physicians both reflect a modest upward trend seen over the past few years.

- Seventy-nine percent of employed and 64 percent of self-employed physicians said they will continue taking new and current Medicare and Medicaid patients, which is up from the prior year's survey.

- Concierge practices stayed level at only three percent, and cash-only practices dropped.

- Participation in accountable care organizations (ACOs) continued to rise from three percent in 2011 to 30 percent in 2015.

- Employed primary-care physicians (PCPs) made an average of $189,000 compared to $212,000 for self-employed physicians. Both of these figures could be impacted by a number of factors in the future, including competing retail clinics, ACO shared savings contracts, payment-reporting websites, CPT code changes and meaningful use penalties.

5 Chronic Disease Prevention and Health Promotion. CDC.gov. http://cdc.gov/chronicdisease/overview
6 Medscape Physician Compensation Report 2015, April 2015. http://www.medscape.com/features/slideshow/compensation/2015/public/overview

When you examine the lay of the land nationally and in your own neighborhood—whether for your strategic plan, your business plan, or your marketing plan—you'll become aware of what concerns people about our healthcare system. This background information is critical to developing effective and creative strategies for addressing the challenges at hand.

ASSESSING YOUR PRACTICE

Several times in this book I've said things have changed, yet they remain the same. Practice assessment is one of the areas in which things really have changed very little. That's primarily because patients' needs haven't changed a lot, with the exception of how powerful the Internet and social media have become. This ubiquitous tool has given patients the ability to communicate with you, as with the world, almost instantly. Furthermore, they expect you to respond in as timely a manner.

You may be asking, "What can I do to make my practice succeed in today's environment?" "How can marketing help me?" "Where do I start?"

You also may ask, "What does a practice assessment have to do with medical marketing?" The answer is: everything. A practice assessment is the vital first step of any effective marketing plan. And it's the answer to the question of where to start. In a very practical sense, you must assess where you are before you can move forward.

SO, HOW DO YOU ASSESS YOUR PRACTICE?

Always begin your practice assessment with an eye toward finding ways to maintain and increase your market share. Start by examining your practice's strengths, weaknesses, opportunities, and threats—what we call SWOT—and by defining your goals. Only after you understand these two elements (SWOT and goals) will you be able to prioritize your marketing challenges.

An effective practice assessment includes a review of both internal and external factors. Internally, this includes things like patient satisfaction data, referral trends, volumes, payer mix, staff surveys and if possible, sources of new patients (i.e., how they heard about your practice).

External assessment includes an analysis of your competitors, the insurance market, employers and the community. As you assess your competitors, try to identify their strengths and weaknesses as well as their branding approach, marketing tactics and messaging in the community. And in your community, identify major employers, key community organizations (i.e., schools, sports leagues, YMCA, etc.), primary referrers (including non-physician sources), and hospital marketing approaches and strategies for your specialty area. Also, list existing healthcare plans as well as those that are entering the community, including Medicaid and Medicare plans.

Always keep in mind that future relationships are being built today. With so many consolidations taking place, the person you work with at one organization today may very well be the same one you'll work with at a different organization tomorrow! Again, that circle of "yes, it's changed, yet it's still the same."

Your assessment should also identify your customers so you can develop and implement appropriate marketing strategies that will meet their needs. Keep in mind the marketing cornerstones: **Access, Availability, Accommodation,** and **Accountability.**

As you assess, you will need to research what your patients want. When it comes to what patients want, there have been countless studies and surveys over the years, and the same considerations continue to appear. Patients want their physicians to:

- Make eye contact
- Smile
- Be on time
- Listen
- Partner with them on care decisions—give them information and the power to make choices
- Honor their values and preferences
- Respect them as persons
- Be honest
- Personalize the care you provide
- Keep them informed
- Coordinate care and help them navigate the increasingly complex healthcare system
- Communicate clearly, especially when giving a diagnosis, treatment or care instructions

- Treat them as a whole person and not just a collection of ailments or symptoms.

- Be accessible—they want to know they can reach you when they need you

- Apologize when you are late or make a mistake

Having learned that, you should implement the following marketing strategies:

- Treat patients as guests.

- Make the most of the technology available to you, including your website, electronic health records, patient portal, etc., yet, keep a personal touch.

- Conduct patient surveys and use the feedback to make meaningful improvements.

- Ensure you have a current and easily accessible patient database with physical and e-mail addresses for practice communication.

- Provide patients with educational resources and information.

- Call selected patients after their visits/procedures.

- Empower all staff to be personable, personal, and accountable.

- Address your patients with appropriate respect.

As you conduct your assessment, you should identify the needs of referral physicians. These include:

- Giving their patients quality care.

- Having patients referred back for care.

- Receiving prompt, informative reports.

- Having referred patients scheduled promptly.

- Having your practice be accountable.

- Educating patients on new treatments, procedures and services.

- Making them feel valued.

This allows you to implement the following strategies:

- Create a database of your referral physicians.

- Keep referrers informed and involved.

- Make it easy for referrers to reach you.

- Offer a dedicated referral phone line.

- Organize a think tank with referrers for difficult cases.

- Develop measurable marketing activities.

- Identify creative and unexpected ways to thank them.

At the end of the day, referral physicians want the **Four A's**, too. They also want cost-effectiveness and demonstrated best practices. See Exhibit 6.1 for sample practice assessment guidelines.

EXHIBIT 6.1 Practice Assessment Guidelines

As you begin your practice assessment, keep in mind these general guidelines. Understand that you must:

- Know who you are.
- Know what you want.
- Know your customers.
- Know what your customers want.
- Know your group and its capabilities.
- Have a plan.
- Implement it on an ongoing basis.
- Know what legal constraints there are on marketing, and structure your plan accordingly.
- Understand that marketing is an evolution of behaviors and layers.
- Write down specific goals.
- Develop basic communication tools.
- Build your brand.
- Hold a strategic planning retreat.
- Support your internal staff and empower them.
- Understand media relations, and use the media as a resource.
- Put yourself in a mindset to lead in your community.
- Recognize the power of customer service.
- Recognize that patients are number one and have a great deal of power.
- Create a list that defines what differentiates your practice and provides value-added opportunities to all your customers.
- Do what you do well, even if you don't do everything.

To address the needs of your health insurance payers, your group might want to consider implementing the following marketing strategies:

- Share your utilization review outcomes.
- Call your insurance contacts at least four times per year.
- Communicate practice differentiation.
- Track patients and revenues.

- Communicate everything in writing.
- Share cost-reduction strategies.
- Get to know administrative personnel.
- Obtain direct marketing approval via your contract.

As you assess the wants and needs of employers, you'll learn that their top priorities are quality, access and pricing. Value purchasing is also important to them, and frequently they're willing to develop direct relationships with providers. Having this knowledge will allow you to implement the following strategies:

- Make contact with current and new community employers.
- Keep employers updated.
- Get to know the benefits managers.
- Create a database, including e-mail addresses for communication/mailings.
- Write articles for company newsletters.
- Invite employers to lunch and to tour your practice.

If you've previously conducted any or all of the assessments I've described, it's a good idea to take another look at them periodically. When you do, be sure to step back and be objective. Evaluate your existing goals to be sure they're still current and that they address what you want for your future.

Examine your mission statement to determine if it's still valid and enumerate the value-added characteristics that differentiate your practice from your competitors. Make sure that your systems have the capability to handle the important operational issues that will arise as your practice matures. See Exhibit 6.2 for a sample practice assessment.

EXHIBIT 6.2 Sample Practice Assessment

Strengths

- Minimal competition (because of creative positioning)
- Good geographic locations
- Strong work ethic
- Willingness to change
- Practice sub specialization
- Strong practice administrator
- Strategic recruiting process
- Belief in marketing

Weaknesses

- Lack of a group mentality
- Lack of vision
- Group apathy
- Inability to make decisions
- Large size (causing the perception of a mill mentality)
- Lack of strong leadership
- Market share not keeping up with community growth
- Lack of marketing

Opportunities

- Join or be a developmental leader in a specialty network.
- Develop a physician panel with the local healthcare coalition.
- Maximize on the health system's strategy to reenergize relations with their medical staff.
- Develop an equity position in a specialty hospital or surgical center.
- Contract to provide services in outlying areas via the use of technology.
- Relocate an existing office with declining census to an area of high residential and commercial growth.
- Review service strategies within the practice and make a commitment to enhance our service approach and implementation.
- Update the practice website to add value for patients.

continued

EXHIBIT 6.2 Sample Practice Assessment

continued

Threats

- Merger of other specialty groups within the region
- Exclusion from physician-developed networks
- Patients seeking treatment where they have easier **Access**
- Patients perceived as giving up "quality" providers in exchange for **Availability** and **Accommodation** at other healthcare outlets such as in pharmacy chains and big box stores.

Value Added or Practice Differentiators

- Physician credentials and training
- Specially credentialed staff
- Location or geographic distribution of office sites
- Operational systems
- Practice capabilities
- Willingness to accept risk
- Global pricing
- Focus on building relationships with payers and employers
- Commitment to a service mentality for customers

Finally, be consistently sensitive to customer service issues throughout all aspects of your assessment.

YOUR AUDIT LIST

As you continue your practice assessment, you should look at the following list to determine your standing in regard to marketing materials and other customer service elements.

- Practice brand-name identity
- Marketing plan or plan of action
- Communication tools
- Relationships
- Competition
- Marketing partners

- Group image
- Public relations
- Community relations
- website and digital strategy
- Promotions for the group
- Mind-set of the group

ASSESSING YOUR PRACTICE IDENTITY

Before implementing your marketing plan, it's also important to make sure your practice has the tools to easily differentiate itself from your competitors and colleagues in the eyes of your community. (See Exhibit 6.3.) Start by reviewing your most fundamental communication tools. Ask yourself the following:

- Do we have a memorable practice name?
- Do we have a graphic identity (logo) that represents what our practice stands for?

These two elements are as basic as it gets when it comes to projecting your desired practice image. And they couldn't be more important to establishing a successful practice identity. Keep in mind that the logo you create is for the ease of recognition for your patients and others who do business with your practice.

As you develop your corporate identity package, plan for the following basic items:

- Logo design
- Letterhead
- Customized #10 envelope
- Business cards
- Note card
- Note card envelope
- Self-stick mailing label
- Appointment card
- Fax cover sheet

Additional printed communication tools you will need in the future may include the following:

- Patient brochure
- Fact sheet template design
- Practice folder
- Physician bio rack card

It's important to create a visual image that allows your patients and other clients to recognize your practice immediately. You want to stand out and differentiate your practice from all of the others who provide care in your specialty and community.

EXHIBIT 6.3 Show How to Differentiate Your Practice

Sometimes physicians and managers tell me they really have a difficult time creating a differentiation list (the "value-added" elements that set their practice apart from others). Because they do the same things everyday, they often don't see their practice as being special or unique to the clients and patients they serve. But look around every time you go shopping. You'll see how easy it is to itemize special attributes.

When patients come to your office, it's very important that you fully and consistently educate them about your products and services. If you survey your patients, you'll probably be amazed to find out how little they're aware of all the products and services provided within your practice. It's especially true in certain specialties such as orthopedics where patients often say they went to a podiatrist because they didn't know an orthopedic group provided foot and ankle care. Or patients who went to a chiropractor because they didn't know their sports medicine doctor's group also took care of backs.

Take time to review your practice and think about all you offer. Write it down. Not only will it help you focus your marketing, it will be of value during your negotiations with hospitals, payers and other physicians.

ASSESSING YOUR LOGO

I believe the quality of your logo design can make a big difference in how potential and current patients look at your practice.

Trademarks and logos make up the most international language in the world. An excellent logo design can cross many barriers and provide your practice with a means of delivering to your patients an unequivocal and uniform message.

Every successful practice has its own "personality," and just as human personalities are complex, so too, is your practice's personality. A successful logo is a means of condensing a complex reality into a single, simple statement—one that can be controlled, modified, developed and matured over time. Your logo needs to be much more than just a distinguishing mark for your practice. It must be an indication of quality, value and reliability.

When considering your logo, keep in mind that it is often your first opportunity to communicate an image for your organization and to create a predisposition in your favor. As you work with an artist or a graphic designer, communicate clearly what you wish to convey. List which words best describe your organization. These are likely to include the following:

- Quality
- Integrity
- Attention to detail
- Professionalism
- Caring
- A practice that is:
  - Up-to-date
  - Efficient
  - Experienced
  - Knowledgeable
  - Conscientious
  - Innovative
  - Friendly, caring
  - Thorough
  - Reliable

Remember these characteristics, as well as the following guidelines, as you work with a designer to develop a logo that truly represents your practice. Your logo should:

- Differentiate your practice from competitors through a distinct identity that contains a minimum of elements.

- Be clear and readable in all sizes, from large (signage) to small (1 to 5 inches or smaller, if needs dictate).

- Be strong enough to stand alone, as required for signage, yet simple enough to have a distinctive presence when other information should stand out (as in print advertising).

- Copy and fax well.

- Reproduce well in color as well as black and white for both high-quality and budget printing projects.

- Translate well on polo shirts, dress shirts, scrubs or lab coats depending on your practice needs.

- Utilize no more than two timeless print styles, based on classic principles of weight, balance and proportion.

EXHIBIT 6.4 Southern Oregon Orthopedic New Logo

Located in Medford, Oregon, Southern Oregon Orthopedics (SOO) is southern Oregon's largest orthopedic surgery group and since 1970, has served the residents of southern Oregon and northern California. The group had been the dominant orthopedic surgery provider in the region with very little competition. However, that was slowly starting to increase. As part of a rebranding effort, they wanted to visually communicate their position as a modern, sophisticated, service-oriented, patient-focused leader in the field of orthopedics and in the Rogue Valley community with a new logo and corporate identity materials. Here are the before and after logos.

Old Logo

New Logo

AN ACCURATE, THOROUGH DIAGNOSIS = A MORE EFFECTIVE TREATMENT PLAN

I've covered a lot of ground in this chapter, and I realize the "homework" I've suggested may seem a bit daunting. But I encourage you to take the time to fully assess your practice. Doing your due diligence to identify and explore your strengths, weaknesses, opportunities and threats as well as to evaluate your brand identity will reap benefits later. It will better equip you to develop effective strategies that capitalize on what makes you different, allowing you to grow and sustain success while also conquering any threats standing in your way.

CHAPTER 7

Engaging Your Team
to be A+ Marketers

Walt Disney once said, "You can design and create, and build the most wonderful place in the world. But it takes people to make the dream a reality."

We've talked about your brand—it is the unique experience people have with your practice. It's the essence of how you deliver healthcare. And as a service-based organization, your employees play an integral role in shaping that customer experience, in making your "dream" practice a reality.

Retail stores and restaurants provide great examples to illustrate this point. How many times have you walked into a store asking about a specific "special" or sale you saw advertised only to have the staff person look back at you with a blank stare, having no clue what you are talking about? Or worse, maybe that staff person argued with you, claiming you must be wrong or mistaken. How did this make you feel? How did this shape your opinion of that retailer? Did it give you confidence in their expertise? Did you feel like a valued customer? Are you likely to still make a purchase there, or are you apt to walk out the door and drive to a competitor? Will you ever go back?

Engaging your team—from physicians and nurses to receptionists, billing and front desk staff—is absolutely critical to the success of any branding effort or marketing plan. And by engage, I mean you must look to them not just as messengers and ambassadors for your practice, but also as valuable resources with unique insight to help you better understand your practice and patients. They may even have untapped ideas to help achieve your goals.

How do you engage your team in marketing?

1. **Involve them early on in the process.** Seek their feedback. They can offer insight from working the "front lines" that you may have never thought of or noticed. Involve them in your SWOT analysis—identifying practice strengths, weaknesses, opportunities and threats—as well as value-added or practice differentiation factors.

2. **Share a draft of the marketing plan with your staff and seek their feedback.** Again, they may have creative ideas to contribute that you overlooked or know of simple tweaks that should be made to the plan so strategies or messages are more effective. Involving them in this part of the process also carries the added benefit of making them feel involved and valued. And employees who feel valued and heard feel a sense of ownership, becoming more personally driven and invested in the success of the organization.

3. **Once the plan is finalized, share it with your team again, as well as the timeline and plans for rolling out specific strategies.** They should be your first target audience. In addition, be sure to arm them with any background information or talking points they may need so that they are informed and can help educate your patients and customers as it relates to your marketing. Staff can even help brainstorm frequently asked questions that patients may have so that you can capture these, as well as formulate responses so that every member of your team feels informed, confident and can respond with a unified voice.

No doubt you want your staff to be warm and welcoming, but you also need them to be knowledgeable and helpful. Again, properly educated, trained and motivated, they can be your very best marketing tool, serving as true ambassadors for your brand.

IDENTIFYING A PHYSICIAN "CHAMPION"

In addition to involving your staff in developing and implementing your marketing plan, physician "buy-in" across your practice is a critical yet sometimes overlooked step.

I've worked with countless medical practices over the past three decades, and I've found the most significant differentiating factor in whether a marketing plan is a document buried somewhere on a desk or is instead a living, breathing action plan that brings about change is identifying and involving a "physician champion." This doctor serves as a key stakeholder, active participant, and advocate in the development and implementation of your marketing plan. You can have the very best practice administrator who gives 100 percent support and fully participates in the marketing planning process yet without physician leadership, support and engagement, it falls flat.

So how do you identify a physician champion within your practice? It does not have to be the most senior physician—although it could be. The characteristics of an effective physician "champion" include the following:

1. **Innovative thinker**—Someone open to new ideas and not afraid of change.

2. **Entrepreneurial mindset**—A physician with some business acumen who isn't afraid to take a creative approach regarding the challenges and opportunities your practice faces.

3. **Respected by his/her peers**—The other physicians in the practice respect this physician's skills, thoughts and opinions.

4. **Action-oriented**—He or she will take on tasks and complete them by deadlines.

5. **Good communicator**—This doctor knows how to educate and motivate the other physicians on the team by speaking to them in terms that are most relevant to them.

6. **Organized**—This physician can be counted on to follow up with partners and collect key information/input from them.

7. **Committed**—He or she will see the process through and make time for meetings.

8. **Motivated**—This physician genuinely likes his or her work and is driven to take action to make it even better.

The physician champion you identify should be involved from the very first marketing planning meeting all the way through implementation. If you have additional physicians who want to be actively involved throughout the process, invite them to attend as well! And if they can't attend meetings, your physician champion can gather their input afterward to synthesize and share with the marketing team.

MARKETING 101

The majority of people working in a medical practice—physicians included—have little to no education about marketing. This is to be expected as their training has typically focused on the delivery of healthcare services. However, since your team needs to play an integral role in your marketing efforts, you must bridge this knowledge gap. The fact that you are reading this book is a great first step! Once you are done, take the initiative and provide your team with a brief "Marketing 101" to get them up to speed. You can do this in a number of ways:

1. **You can share this book with others on your team.** This is an easy way for you to share and educate others in your group. You could even have some fun with it and hold a "book club" session to discuss what everyone has learned and any ideas their reading stimulated. This could be an enjoyable staff/team-building event, or it could be incorporated into existing physician or team meetings already on the schedule.

2. **Craft a PowerPoint or Keynote presentation based on the fundamental tenets you have learned.** I have done this for a number of my clients, especially new clients who are trying to engage their physician leadership in the marketing process. Don't make it *Gone with the Wind*. Hit the high points and those most relevant to your specific audience. Key things to cover:

    ○ The role of the "prosumer"

    ○ Marketing is more than ads and brochures; it includes relationships, service, community and communication.

    ○ Relationship and referral development

    ○ Fostering a culture of gratitude

    ○ The importance of service and **The Four A's—Access, Availability, Accountability** and **Accommodation**

    ○ Patient expectations for personalized care

    ○ Community involvement, including how staff can play a role

    ○ The rise and impact of technology and social media

3. **Bring in an outside speaker or consultant to share this information.** Look for someone experienced in the nuances of healthcare marketing, especially managing customer service and referral development.

MAINTAINING ONGOING COMMUNICATION AND EDUCATION

Engaging your team to be A+ marketers is not just a one-time thing. The most successful practices I have worked with make this an ongoing effort.

It begins with new hires and orientation to your practice. This needs to go beyond the usual HR policies and practice procedures. Educate them about your brand promise, share your current marketing plan, and inform them about your expectations for their support in communicating and carrying out key strategies. Consider having your strongest employee or physician ambassador participate in this process and help orient new hires by sharing personal experiences and examples of how he or she lives out the marketing plan.

Ensure new physicians and employees know your mission, vision and values. Share the history of your practice—how it was founded, how it has grown, guiding principles, innovations and community involvement. This builds a solid foundation from the start and makes new hires feel a part of something greater than just themselves. They feel connected to a special, respected group with deep roots and ties within the community.

Equip all new hires with background information and answers to commonly asked questions. And if they encounter a question they don't know the answer to, empower them to go to someone who can assist.

In addition, help new staff members to better understand your target audience and primary patient base, including their demographics, unique characteristics, top concerns or issues, etc. For example, if you are an ophthalmology practice, help the new staff understand that many of your patients come into your office with vision issues and can't read smaller type. These patients may have challenges and need assistance with reading forms, signs or paperwork, or even navigating their way through the office. Or if you are an orthopedic practice, patients coming to you may be in great pain and need assistance walking back to the exam room. Or perhaps you care for patients with arthritis who may have trouble grasping things and need a fatter pen to write with, assistance with a restroom door handle, etc. Help your team to understand and think through the little things because those can make the biggest difference in building strong patient relationships and loyalty. By investing in sharing this information on the front end, you help to establish and foster a culture where a staff member sees his or her role as more of a career or calling rather than just another job.

Beyond a thorough orientation process, you need to periodically check to ensure your branding is being carried out as expected—an audit of sorts. Review all practice signs, forms and handouts. Browse through your website and check all links. Examine any materials available in your waiting or exam rooms and make sure they are current. Pull anything that isn't. Shadow each department and review how phone calls and patient interactions are being handled.

Check in with your team members as well. Several times a year, in staff or department meetings, seek their input. What is working? What isn't? Any new issues to be addressed? Any significant feedback from interactions or experiences with patients? Any new ideas they have to address practice challenges or take advantage of new opportunities? How well do they think **The Four A's—Access, Availability, Accommodation** and **Accountability**—are being implemented?

As your practice changes—new physicians, new hours, new locations, new services or treatments, a new marketing strategy or campaign—make sure your staff are the first to know. Give them the background information they need to support the change and your marketing efforts. If you have acquired a new facility or piece of equipment, give them the first "sneak peek" tour. Share with them any new marketing tools—website changes, blogs, brochures, ads, etc., before they hit the marketplace.

Again, your physicians and staff are perhaps the most significant part of your brand. If you invest in their orientation and ongoing education, seek their ideas and input, empower them with answers and information, it will pay off well.

CHAPTER 8

Telling Your Story—Practical Approaches to Media Relations and Advertising

THE DIFFERENCE BETWEEN ADVERTISING AND PUBLIC RELATIONS

"Advertising is what you pay for; publicity (or public relations) is what you pray for," goes an old business saying.

That may seem a simplistic explanation, but it is actually a pretty easy way to remember the difference between advertising and public relations. Over the years, I have run across many healthcare professionals who think marketing, public relations and advertising are all the same thing, and they use these terms interchangeably. While they are certainly related and should be integrated, they are also very different.

Here are four primary ways advertising and public relations (PR) differ:

1. **Paid vs. Free**—With advertising, you pay to create and deliver your message or ad. This can be through a variety of media, including print, radio, billboard, TV and online. Public relations, by contrast, is known as "free" or "earned" media. It is when a third party or media outlet delivers your message or "story" through an article, editorial or news segment. It typically results from a strategic process of building relationships with key

stakeholders, including reporters at media outlets, and sharing announcements or news stories through a news release or media pitch.

2. **Credibility**—When your message is shared through a news story, it typically has more credibility than an ad because it comes from a third-party journalist, who by publishing or broadcasting it, has independently verified the content and is providing an endorsement of sorts. This can be quite effective in shaping public opinion. On the other hand, when people see an advertisement, they know it was created and purchased by a business trying to sell them a product or service, so it is telling them what that business wants them to see or hear. Think of it this way: with advertising, you are telling someone how great you are; with PR, someone else not affiliated with your practice or organization in any way is lifting you up as a valued resource and sharing in their own words how great you are. That can have a positive impact on your brand awareness and perception.

3. **Control**—With advertising, you have control over the content as well as where and when it will appear in the media because you have paid for it. With public relations, you share your message or story idea with a media outlet and give up control over the actual final message as well as if and when it will appear. They can choose to edit it down or change it, run with it or not even use it at all.

4. **Frequency**—With advertising, you can run your ad as many times and for as long as your budget will allow. With public relations, however, you can only submit a news release about a specific event or topic once to a reporter. In addition, any media coverage you receive will typically only air once with the exception that many media outlets will include the story on their websites for a period of time after it appears. You can also extend a media story's shelf life by including it on your own website and social media, e-mailing it to patients or key contacts, or sharing copies of printed stories in your waiting or exam rooms as well as in any marketing packets you use for community events, talks or referral visits.

In addition to the differences described above, public relations is broader than simply media relations. It encompasses a number of different tools and outlets. You can certainly distribute a press release to a targeted publication, website or broadcast station to try to share a message with your target audience. However, you can also share that same message through a personal letter or e-mail, an organization e-newsletter, in a blog post, at a community presentation or even through informative posts on your social media channels (and don't forget to share it with your employee team, too!).

As you formulate your marketing plan, be sure to explore both advertising and public relations opportunities to determine the right combination to achieve your specific goals. Now we'll dig a little deeper into effective media relations.

GENERATING POSITIVE MEDIA COVERAGE

To succeed in generating positive media coverage for your physicians and practice, you must take on the roles of resource and storyteller. First, you must position your physicians and practice as expert resources. Identify your local media outlets—newspaper, TV stations, news radio, community magazines, etc. Determine who covers medical or health-related issues at each. Then reach out to introduce yourself, your physicians and your practice and offer to serve as a resource for any media stories that might relate to your area of specialty. Highlight any special knowledge, credentials or experience they have. Media is an industry that has seen revolutionary change in the past decade. As a result, there are fewer reporters, and they are increasingly dependent on others for content. If you can earn their trust as a valued resource, your practice can reap the benefits. And how do you earn that trust? In much the same way you do with your patients and referral sources—**The Four A's**—be **Accessible**, **Available** (and responsive), **Accommodating** and **Accountable**.

Keep in mind that reporters work on deadline. If they can't get what they need from you in the timeframe they need it, they will go to someone else, possibly even your competitor. Here are a few general tips on media interviews and working with reporters:

1. **Avoid using industry jargon or medical lingo.** Speak in terms the general public will understand just as you would with a patient or caregiver.

2. **Keep your responses brief.** Master the art of speaking in sound bites.

3. **If you're asked a question and you don't know the answer, offer to get back in touch with the reporter after you've gathered more information.** Remember that reporters have deadlines, so be sure to find out when that deadline is and call back before then.

In addition to serving as a resource, you need to think as a reporter yourself to maximize media opportunities for your practice. Start by identifying opportunities to share news. These can come in many forms—a "special" patient story, introducing a new physician, opening a new office, being "first" to do a procedure in your community, or leading a community relations effort tied to preventive healthcare just to name a few. In addition, keep your ear out for other current medical or health headlines and determine if your physicians can provide a local angle or perspective. These can be stories on disease outbreaks, medical breakthroughs, new or emerging health or treatment trends, or maybe a celebrity who's benefited from (or died from) something that one of your physicians has extensive knowledge about or expertise in. Reporters are frequently looking for a local angle or expert on a national story.

Now that you've identified opportunities, you need to become a storyteller. Present the problem or issue, supported with facts, and then your unique solution. Think and speak in terms of impact and direct benefits to the patient or consumer (i.e., less side effects, quicker recovery time, etc.), and make it human. If the story features a new treatment or procedure, tie in a patient's story or experience, including direct quotes to help the reader connect.

HOW TO PITCH YOUR STORY

So you have identified a great story. What next? Once you have gathered all of the necessary details, the next step is to craft a news release. A news release or press release is a concise, compelling document designed to share your news with targeted media. I've included a sample in Exhibit 8.1. Feel free to use it as a guide. To help make your press release effective and stand out from the crowd, you should:

1. **Attract attention with a compelling headline** (which can also become your subject line when e-mailing it to a reporter). It should focus on the meat of your story (the problem solved or event happening).

2. **Keep it brief and factual.** Aim for one page or a maximum of two. Get right to the point. Focus in on the Who, What, When, Where and Why. And don't make it a promotional piece. Again, this is not an ad. Certainly your physicians and practice will be woven into the story, but the story itself must stand on its own.

3. **Write it in third person** as if you are a reporter with no ties to the story. It should not be promotional in nature.

4. **Incorporate relevant background statistics** from reputable sources to support your story.

5. **Include quotes.** This helps to give your story a human dimension and added credibility. Choose someone with close ties to the story. Depending on the nature of the story, this can be one of your physicians, a patient, or someone respected within your field or community.

6. **Be sure to proofread.** Have it proofed several times by several different people, including someone who knows nothing about the story and can provide honest feedback. The quickest way for you to lose credibility and have your release not get covered is for a reporter to see a grammatical or spelling error.

7. **Include any relevant links**, including your website and any other resources cited.

8. **Don't forget to include your contact information**—name, a direct phone number (preferably cell phone) and e-mail address.

Now you've crafted the perfect press release. It is time to distribute it and pitch your story. How do you do that?

1. **Know the right media outlet(s) and reporter(s).** This is where that relationship-building helps. Don't blanket the media. Make sure the reporters and outlets you are targeting are the right fit. If you are a pediatric practice and one of your physicians is one of the first in the area to offer a new service or treatment, there is no point in sending it to the local senior magazine.

2. **Familiarize yourself with the reporter's former work.** Read through his or her recent stories. Then look at your story through the reporter's eyes and help draw the connection to its relevance.

3. **Customize your pitch based on the specific media outlet and address the reporter by name.** This goes back to building relationships just like you do with your patients and referral sources. If a reporter has done a story on a similar topic or issue, reference how your story complements that one and could build on past work.

4. **Be concise.** Get straight to the point.

5. **E-mail first. Call later.** And respect their response. If you don't hear back, don't keep calling.

6. **Include your contact information and offer to assist** with questions, additional information, high-quality photos/video (if you have them) or setting up interviews.

7. **Don't pit media against each other** or try to convince an outlet to cover you by mentioning that another one already did. That will actually work to your disadvantage. Just like you have competitors, they do, too.

8. **Make sure your story is relevant.** Don't flood the media with news releases or pitches. Not everything that is important to your practice is news. For example, your practice may offer a new treatment, but if you are not the first in the community to offer that treatment, it will not be newsworthy for a media outlet. That shouldn't stop you from sharing news through other channels you control—like your website, a patient e-mail or letter, etc.

9. **Provide advanced notice.** Make sure you are giving a reporter plenty of lead time before an event or product/service launch. This allows them to block time, prepare and do any needed background research.

10. **As mentioned before**, a press release may or may not get picked up by the media. Sometimes a larger news story takes precedence and consumes media coverage for a period of time. And sometimes a reporter just doesn't see a topic as newsworthy. That's not to say that communicating through releases isn't still an important part of your public relations efforts. Don't be discouraged, and don't abandon this approach.

A REAL-LIFE MEDIA RELATIONS SUCCESS STORY

Established in 1966 and based in Dallas, Texas Retina Associates is a large ophthalmology sub-specialty practice. At the time, they had 13 offices stretched from Waco to Lubbock to Wichita Falls. Their physician team had participated in more than 75 national clinical trials over a period of nearly three decades, including many in partnership with an independent, non-profit research center called the Retina Foundation of the Southwest. Both organizations had experienced tremendous growth and needed to expand capacity in Dallas.

Since the two had worked so closely together, they decided to explore the possibility of building new offices under the same roof that were custom-designed for optimal patient care and research utility. The goal was to serve as a national model for patient-centered medical research by providing patients with more immediate, expanded and direct access to breakthrough treatments and clinical trials at this first-of-its-kind facility. Although still independent of each other, being under the same roof would allow them to work more collaboratively and efficiently, attracting additional research studies to the Dallas community, especially from pharmaceutical companies developing promising new treatments.

We developed a targeted news release (see Exhibit 8.1) and media strategy to share this news both locally and throughout the medical community. The story received great coverage as you can see in 8.2.

EXHIBIT 8.1 Texas Retina Associates Dallas Office News Release

FOR IMMEDIATE RELEASE: February 14, 2013

Media Contacts:

Jeff Brockette, Texas Retina Associates
214-692-6941/jbrockette@texasretina.com
Fran Crawford, Texas Retina Associates
214-692-6941/fcrawford@texasretina.com
Jean Buys, Retina Foundation of the Southwest
214-363-3911 x109/jbuys@retinafoundation.org

Texas Retina Associates and Retina Foundation of the Southwest Open New Dallas Offices, Serve as a National Model for Patient-Centered Medical Research

DALLAS, TX—Two of the country's leading eye research institutions founded and based in Dallas—Texas Retina Associates (TRA) and the Retina Foundation of the Southwest (RFSW)—have recently opened new offices under the same roof. The new facilities are located at 9600 N. Central Expressway in Dallas, at the southeast corner of N. Central Expressway and Walnut Hill Lane in Central Dallas, and were custom designed to meet the needs of each organization.

While separate, TRA physicians and RFSW scientists have worked closely together for more than 30 years to identify new treatments for retina conditions such as age-related macular degeneration, diabetic retinopathy, retinitis pigmentosa and uveitis—leading causes of vision loss in millions of people throughout the world. The goal of sharing this recently renovated building is to provide patients with more immediate, expanded and direct access to breakthrough treatments and clinical trials for these retina conditions and many others. Both facilities were custom-designed for optimal patient care and research utility.

About TRA and RFSW

Established in 1966, Texas Retina Associates, with 13 offices throughout the state and 17 retina-fellowship-trained physicians, is Texas' largest, most experienced ophthalmology practice focused specifically on the diagnosis and medical and surgical management of diseases of the retina and vitreous. The practice's sub-specialized physician team has participated in more than 75 national clinical trials over the past 20 years, bringing the newest retina and vitreous treatments to its patients.

Also based in Dallas, the Retina Foundation of the Southwest is an independent, non-profit research institute established in 1982. The Foundation has grown into one of the leading independent vision research centers in the United States, with a staff of 28 dedicated to finding the causes, treatments and potential cures for numerous eye diseases that cause severe visual impairment. Patients are referred by ophthalmologists from Dallas and around the U.S. and even the world. Because the center is funded by philanthropic support and research grants, patients receive care at no cost.

continued

EXHIBIT 8.1 Texas Retina Associates Dallas Office News Release

continued

A New Model for Medical Research

Even though Texas Retina Associates and the Retina Foundation of the Southwest are separate organizations with separate doors, leaders of both have shared close ties for years and believe that being under the same roof will allow them to work more collaboratively and efficiently, attracting additional research studies to the Dallas community, especially from pharmaceutical companies developing promising new treatments.

Karl Csaky, M.D., Ph.D., serves as a vitreoretinal specialist at TRA as well as the T. Boone Pickens Senior Scientist and Director of the Molecular Ophthalmology Laboratory at the RFSW.

"In the last five to 10 years, as medicine has become more efficient, a void has emerged in patient-oriented research," explains Dr. Csaky. "Many of the traditional academic research institutions have been forced to cut back, and they also face great challenges in meeting pharmaceutical companies' demands for efficiency. Moving Texas Retina Associates and the Retina Foundation of the Southwest into the same building allows us to operate even more efficiently than we have been. We will be better able to meet those demands, and we can more quickly and easily translate research from the lab to patient care. I think others are going to look to us as a new model to replicate across the country."

Retina Foundation of the Southwest Chief Scientific and Executive Officer David G. Birch, M.D., concurs. "We are one of the only independent eye research facilities in the world and a key player in the international effort to combat severe visual impairment," he said. "Our independence from a major medical institution gives us tremendous flexibility to respond to new opportunities in research and fluctuations in funding."

Another primary reason for the move was to ease convenience for patients who are involved in clinical trials through both organizations, allowing them to receive all the care, testing and treatment they need in the same building.

Dallas—An Epicenter of Emerging Developments in Retina Care

While the field of retina care and research has evolved tremendously in the past 20 years, both TRA and RFSW leaders believe they still have a lot of work to do.

"In our field, there are so many unmet needs, and as a physician, one of the most frustrating things is to have to tell a patient there is nothing we can do," said Dr. Csaky. "Now we have a facility that allows us to push the envelope on our knowledge and understanding of retina diseases, as well as how to treat those conditions in the most efficient manner."

TRA vitreoretinal specialist and RFSW board member David Callanan, M.D., also believes the new proximity between the two organizations will allow each to maximize their strengths to improve sight preservation. "There are more than 100 different ophthalmology diseases that affect the retina, and many of the current treatments are woefully inadequate," he explains. "Patients are desperate for new and better treatments, and through our combined efforts, we hope to attract even more trials to the Greater Dallas community, especially the early Phase 1 and Phase 2 trials."

continued

EXHIBIT 8.1 Texas Retina Associates Dallas Office News Release

continued

A couple of the most exciting collaborative research developments in progress include:

1. A more in-depth understanding of what exactly is wrong in patients with age-related macular degeneration and how anatomical retina changes affect their vision. Dallas-based research is focused on developing more specialized tests that measure the earliest retina function and anatomy changes beyond just basic vision such as how the retina functions in dim light. This will allow retina physicians to create more individualized treatments as well as more rapid assessments.
2. New drug delivery devices and implants such as a contact lens that can deliver time-released medication directly to the eye, avoiding many of the systemic issues associated with drugs that must travel through the bloodstream.

In addition, the RFSW is one of the only centers conducting FDA-approved research with adult stem cells that could lead to a fundamental change in how physicians approach atrophic age-related macular degeneration.

Learn More

For further information about Texas Retina Associates, visit www.texasretina.com or call 214-692-6941. For the Retina Foundation, call 214-363-3911 or visit www.retinafoundation.org. Both organizations will hold an open house for the medical community on Sunday, February 24, 2013, from 2:00 - 4:00 pm. If you are interested in attending, please RSVP by February 20 to rsvp@texasretina.com.

ADDITIONAL BACKGROUND:
Past Groundbreaking Medical Eye Research Conducted in Dallas

In addition to clinical trials that have contributed to advances in treatment for macular and retinal disease, past groundbreaking discoveries from the Retina Foundation of the Southwest include:

- Discovered that DHA in mother's milk is necessary for infant eye and brain development. Enhanced formula containing DHA is now sold worldwide.
- Proved that cataracts should be removed in infants to enable normal visual development
- Discovered the function of the gene that causes Stargardt disease (juvenile macular degeneration)
- Discovered that blue light can cause damage to the eyes and lead to macular degeneration
- One of seven research institutes in the world pioneering the ARGUS II Retinal Prosthesis System -- an implant in the eye designed to provide a low level of stimulation of vision for patients who are blind.
- Pioneered improvements in visual testing for retinitis pigmentosa and allied retinal degenerations
- Developed an inexpensive distance stereoacuity test, the Randot test, for children as young as three years of age to monitor kids with intermittent exotropia (when one eye drifts out). Changes in distance stereoacuity over time may signal deterioration and the need for surgical correction to re-align the eyes.

EXHIBIT 8.2 Texas Medical Association's *"Me & My Doctor"* Blog Article on New Texas Retina Associates Dallas Office

TEXAS MEDICAL ASSOCIATION

ABOUT US   CONTACT   GUEST POST

Me&My Doctor
join the discussion

Home | Hot Topics | Red Tape | Hey, Doc (ACA) | Medicare and Medicaid | Public Health | Final Decisions

WEDNESDAY, APRIL 3, 2013

Dallas Sight-saving Organizations Establish National Model for Patient-centered Medical Research

Karl Csaky, M.D., Ph.D.

As a physician, one of the most frustrating things is to tell a patient there is nothing we can do. We know patients are desperate for new and better treatments.

In order to pioneer new treatments for many blinding eye diseases like age-related macular degeneration, two of the country's leading eye research institutions founded and based in Dallas -- Texas Retina Associates (TRA) and the Retina Foundation of the Southwest (RFSW) -- recently moved into new offices under the same roof. This arrangement is unique among clinics in the United States and will allow researchers and clinicians at the two institutions to work more closely together, finding cures for many retinal diseases for which there are no effective treatments. For example, ongoing research in dry age-related macular degeneration allows for patients suffering from this disease to have renewed hope.

An example of this type of collaborative work led to the U.S. Food and Drug Administration's approval of the Argus II Retinal Prosthesis treatment for blind patients. The Argus II is an implant that allows images, which are captured by a camera on glasses to be transmitted to the brain, thus allowing the brain to perceive patterns of light corresponding to the captured images. The RFSW was one of seven

continued

EXHIBIT 8.2 Texas Medical Association's *"Me & My Doctor"* Blog Article on New Texas Retina Associates Dallas Office

continued

II device in providing sight for blind patients and continues to partner with Second Sight Medical Products to refine and advance this revolutionary technology. The RFSW's Chief Scientific and Executive Director David Birch, Ph.D., was the principal investigator of the Dallas site, and TRA's Rand Spencer, M.D., was the surgeon.

TRA physicians and RFSW scientists have worked closely together for more than 30 years to identify new treatments like this for many of the leading causes of vision loss in millions of people throughout the world.

In the last five to 10 years, as medicine has become more efficient, a void has emerged in patient-oriented research. Many of the traditional academic research institutions have been forced to cut back, and they also face great challenges in meeting the demands for efficiency. The new shared TRA/RFSW facility allows us to better meet those demands, attract additional clinical trials, and more quickly and easily translate research from the lab to patient care. It is allowing us to push the envelope on our knowledge and understanding of retina diseases, as well as how to best treat those conditions. This type of research partnership is a new model that I believe many others will look to replicate across the country.

Karl Csaky, M.D., Ph.D., serves as a vitreoretinal specialist at Texas Retina Associates as well as the T. Boone Pickens Senior Scientist and Director of the Molecular Ophthalmology Laboratory at the Retina Foundation of the Southwest.

CRISIS COMMUNICATION TIPS

Unfortunately, not all news is good news, and interactions with the media can also occur in crisis situations. Crisis communication could warrant its own chapter or book, but I'll just touch on a few primary tenets here. The single greatest thing to remember is to expect the unexpected. The more you think through and prepare for things that could go wrong in your practice or organization, the better equipped you will be to handle them and protect your reputation and brand.

Here are a few general tips. Again, I am just touching the tip of the iceberg. Also, depending on the nature of the crisis, I would encourage you to consult with your attorney and if necessary, a crisis communication expert.

1. **Acknowledge what happened.** Don't ever lie.

2. **Respond quickly.** The longer you wait, the more damage you may face.

3. **Stick to the facts.** Don't embellish or offer speculation or opinions on what has happened.

4. **Identify a spokesperson.** This person should be someone with proper, formal media training. All communication regarding the crisis should filter through this person.

5. **Don't say, "no comment."** Too often, saying this is, at best, perceived as ignorance and, at worst, as admission of guilt.

6. **Don't speak "off the record."** Nothing said to a reporter is ever really off the record. Be prepared for anything you say to be used.

7. **Show compassion.** Express genuine concern and empathy for the victim(s) of the crisis.

8. **Be forthcoming.** This means the good, the bad and the ugly. Don't try to bury the bad—it will eventually get out.

9. **Talk solutions.** Communicate actions that are being taken to remedy the situation and prevent it from occurring again.

MAKING THE MOST OF TARGETED ADVERTISING

We've talked a lot about PR or "earned" media. Now let's talk about how to make the most of "paid" media, better known as advertising.

While news media coverage has the highest credibility, the only way to guarantee complete control of your specific message is through paid advertising. Depending on your practice goals and budget, this can be an effective way to communicate your message to your target audience.

IDENTIFYING THE BEST MEDIA

Many who are new to marketing (and even some who aren't) often jump in with a pie-in-the-sky attitude. They want an ad in the major local newspaper, billboards, a drive-time radio blitz or a television commercial. These mediums all have a place in the marketing world (albeit a decreasing one in many markets), but they also come with high price tags and often are not the best approach for a small business like a medical practice, especially with a limited budget.

What I have found to be most effective for the practices we have worked with is targeted advertising with local community or niche publications. These can include neighborhood magazines, small-town or senior-focused newspapers, and larger employee newsletters/magazines. This allows you to deliver a targeted message—whether it be announcing a new office, accepting a new health plan, welcoming a new physician, or promoting a specific service—more directly to the people you wish to reach. Many of these publications even have special issues with a health and wellness focus or local medical directory that makes sense for your specific goals.

If you are considering adding advertising into your marketing plan, here are a few things to keep in mind:

1. **Size**—For print publications, I don't recommend running anything smaller than 1/4 page and actually prefer a 1/2 page or larger ad. Anything smaller simply gets lost on the page.

2. **Frequency**—I typically recommend at least a three-time run. People often have to see a message several times before they retain it.

3. **Timing**—Explore the media outlet's editorial calendar. Are there specific issues or months that make more sense for your practice based on their editorial focus or target demographic?

CREATING YOUR AD

Whether you work with a design professional, agency or media outlet to create your ad, here are a few tips to keep in mind. These are primarily for print or online ads, but some of the general suggestions apply to radio and TV as well.

- Make sure you use a single, targeted key message. Don't try to communicate everything in one ad.

- Craft concise, creative and compelling content to support your key message. Again, keep it brief and to the point.

- Don't be afraid of white space. A clean design actually helps your ad stand out from the clutter and draws the reader's eye to the content.

- Use photos or graphics. A picture can truly be worth a thousand words. Just make sure you use one that is unique and relatable for your target audience. While stock photography is inexpensive, it is also overused, and a competitor's ad could wind up using the exact same image.

- Keep the tone of the ad warm and friendly. Too many healthcare ads feel stiff, formal and "corporate."

- Don't use too many fonts or type styles. Again, keep it clean. And be sure the type size is large enough to be easily read, especially if you are targeting seniors.

- Always include a prominent call to action. This is usually a phone number but can also include an e-mail address or website. The eye travels from the upper left down to the lower right, so it is best to place your call to action in the lower right quadrant of your ad.

NEGOTIATING ADDED VALUE

When you are working with a local media organization to purchase advertising, you need to put your own sales hat on and embrace the power of negotiation. You are making a deal, and you want to ensure you are maximizing the value you receive from that deal. Even if a media outlet won't negotiate on cost, there are often other assets they have available that could help you to further reach your goals.

One of the first things I encourage medical practices to explore if they are purchasing print advertising in neighborhood publications is editorial columns. Not all, but some publications can provide the opportunity for one of your physicians or healthcare professionals to contribute an article or column on a timely health topic or one that coincides with their editorial focus for that issue. This allows you to gain a public relations opportunity in addition to your advertising. The article typically appears in the same issue as your ad but is completely separate. And like any article, it must be non-promotional in approach, meaning it is strictly an informational article on a specific health topic without any reference within the piece to your practice or physician(s) other than a byline.

In the byline, the publication will typically list the author, credentials and practice name/affiliation. Sometimes they will allow you to add a phone number, e-mail or website to this byline as well. By running an ad and having an article in the same publication, you are layering your marketing efforts and increasing the strength of your branding message.

A second common value-added item to negotiate is online advertising on a media outlet's website. As you know, people are increasingly turning to online sources for news, and local/community news is no exception. If you are meeting with a sales representative about print or broadcast media advertising, be sure to ask if you can secure an online ad on their website as well. Then be sure to create an online ad that complements your primary print or broadcast ad so that you are once again reinforcing your message and layering your marketing.

Finally, some media outlets also sponsor key community events like health fairs, family events, baby fairs, senior expos, children's events or women's expos. If the media outlet you are working with is involved in an event that also reaches your target market, ask if, as a part of your advertising agreement, you can participate in that event perhaps as a speaker, with a booth or table, or even if they will distribute your printed materials.

A REAL-LIFE ADVERTISING EXAMPLE

One of our clients, Physician Associates, a large, multi-specialty group practice focused on primary care with multiple offices throughout the community, had recently been acquired by one of the large local health systems. This acquisition was designed to enhance coordination of care and also provide patients with increased access to specialists and specialty facilities.

With more than 90 physicians practicing family medicine, internal medicine, pediatrics, pediatric gastroenterology, obstetrics and gynecology, orthopedics and podiatry, Physician Associates knew that just like all politics are local, people think more in terms of their own personal, neighborhood physician than they do a large healthcare network. The practice wanted to maintain its reputation for providing warm, friendly, high-quality, personalized care at the neighborhood level. To that end, we focused all of their advertising on select community publications and generated ads that through the graphics and copy, conveyed this approach. We also carried this "neighborhood" design through to their other printed materials, including neighborhood physician directories, individual physician bio rack cards and even the PowerPoint template their physicians used for presentations to community groups. See Exhibit 8.3 for ad examples.

EXHIBIT 8.3 Physician Associates Community Ads

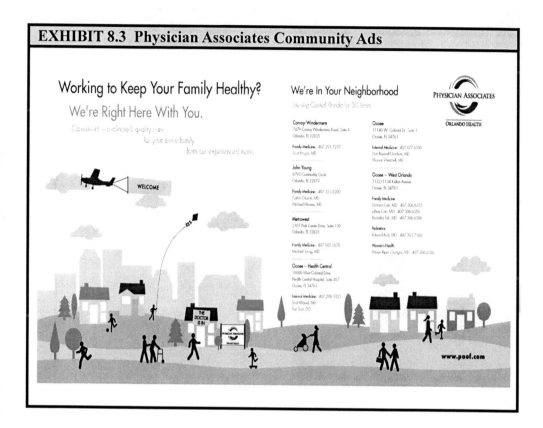

EXHIBIT 8.3 Physician Associates Community Ads (continued)

PHYSICIAN ASSOCIATES

ORLANDO HEALTH

Good Health from Our Family to Yours

Your Partner on the Journey to Optimum Health

Penny Danna, MD, FACOG
Board Certified in Obstetrics and Gynecology

Warmly welcoming new patients!

Conveniently located in Baldwin Park, Dr. Danna is devoted to caring for the special needs of women through all stages of life, from puberty through menopause.

- Testosterone pellet therapy for women
- Total and high-risk pregnancy care
- Well-woman exams
- Hormone replacement therapy
- Menopause care

Same-day appointments available!

Baldwin Park
867 Outer Road, Suite A
Orlando, Florida 32814
407-898-6588

www.paof.com

EXHIBIT 8.3 Physician Associates Community Ads (continued)

EXHIBIT 8.4 Texas Retina Associates New Physician Ad for Lubbock Newspaper

EXHIBIT 8.5 JLR Center for Pain Medicine CIGNA Ad in Walt Disney World's Employee Magazine *Eyes and Ears*

TELLING YOUR STORY—MORE THAN A PRETTY PICTURE

… or powerful prose. Some practices think that their brand is based on a great logo, a catchy slogan or a flashy ad. What they don't realize is that their brand is really how they are perceived by patients and customers. It is the feeling people get when they leave your office, when they hang up the phone after calling to make an appointment or ask a question, when they receive your e-mail or letter. And nothing is worse than false advertising or an empty promise which is exactly what you deliver if your patient's (or referring physician's or vendor's) experience doesn't match up to the pretty picture or clever caption. On the flip side, delight others with your service and then communicate and reinforce this "brand" with effective storytelling. Now you are on your way to a position of market leadership.

WHEN YOU ARE NOT YOUR TARGET AUDIENCE

"I don't get it."

"It's too feminine."

"It doesn't speak to me."

This kind of reaction may mean it is back to the drawing board ... or it may be perfectly fine. The question here is: Who are you trying to reach?

In healthcare, more often than not, your number one target audience is the female head of household who is the healthcare decision-maker for her family. So if you are a male physician or practice administrator, and the latest ad for your practice doesn't resonate with you, that may be okay as long as your target audience reacts and responds favorably. Gather a focus group for your targeted marketing—formal or informal—and test it out. It could be as simple as gathering staff, friends, family or neighbors. You not "getting it" may even be exactly what your practice needs.

ACCESS AND ACCOMMODATION—TYPESTYLE MATTERS

Whether it's for a local community publication ad, a patient handout or your website, type size can make or break the effectiveness of your marketing and communication efforts.

Fonts and type sizes that are easy on the eye of a 30-year-old can be impossible to read for someone 45 or older. Here are a few rules to keep in mind as you create pieces for your practice:

1. Avoid reverse type (white or light type on dark background) as much as possible, especially on websites and in the main body copy of an ad, flyer or brochure.
2. Use serif type (i.e., Times Roman, Georgia) for printed materials. Sans serif fonts like Helvetica or Arial are fine for headlines but harder to read in large blocks of type.
3. Allow plenty of white space.
4. Make sure everything is at least 12- to 14-point type. If you use a font that tends to run small, you may need to bump this up.
5. Use bold, underline and italics sparingly. These are great for adding emphasis, but should be the exception not the rule.

CHAPTER 9

Reaching Out—A Guide to Community Relations

English poet Alfred, Lord Tennyson once said, "I am a part of all that I have met."

When we discuss the cornerstones of marketing, The **Four A's—Access, Availability, Accountability**, and **Accommodation**, we're not only talking about the relationship a patient has with your practice. In addition to the connection a patient has with a direct referral from another physician, family, or friend, you can position your practice and physicians as leaders by your integration with your community.

In fact, you are your community, and building positive, mutually beneficial relationships with your "neighbors" is key to your success. It not only generates awareness, sparks opportunities and stimulates new business for your practice, it builds equity in your community "bank account." It positions you as a leader, fostering confidence and credibility among both your current patients and referring physicians (who are also your best sources for new patients) as well as those who are just getting to know you.

Not to mention community relations is fun and rewarding! It anchors your practice and brings pride and team-building opportunities to your staff. It's also some of the best positioning you can do. So where do you start?

IDENTIFYING THE RIGHT ORGANIZATIONS

This will vary depending on your specialty and target audience. For a pediatric practice, you might want to align with the local elementary school, nearby pre-schools and daycares, PTAs or area Mom's groups and clubs. If, on the other hand, you are a cataract surgeon trying to reach older adults, you need to explore opportunities with senior clubs and centers. Several orthopedic groups that specialize in sports medicine reach out to provide their expertise and services to athletic teams at the youth, high school, college and even professional levels. And if your target audience is more broad, it might make sense to join the local Rotary Club or Chamber of Commerce to network with business professionals in your community. The opportunities are as endless as your creativity. Here is a list of some of the types of organizations I've seen medical practices successfully align with over the years:

- YMCA

- Rotary

- Chamber of Commerce, including smaller community chambers

- Women's organizations

- Sports leagues or teams—youth, amateur, school and professional

- Schools—including preschools and elementary schools as well as high schools and colleges

- Churches and religious organizations (i.e., Jewish Community Center)

- Large employers—can participate in employee health or open enrollment fairs, speak at lunch 'n' learn programs, contribute an article for their wellness newsletter, etc.

- Nonprofit organizations—could relate to your specialty (i.e., an ophthalmology practice supporting Prevent Blindness, an OB/GYN working with March of Dimes, a cardiology practice participating in the annual Heart Walk), but doesn't have to. You may choose to support an organization that fills a more general community need like your local food bank or homeless shelter or one for which you or your partners or staff have a personal passion or connection.

ENGAGE

So you have identified some possible organization(s) to associate with, now what? You must engage. Simply making an introduction or paying a membership is not enough. You must become involved. This could include serving on a committee, volunteering for an event, lending financial or in-kind support, making a presentation or writing an article just to name a few ideas. Get to know the organization's leadership, find out what they need most, and then work with your physician partners and staff to determine how you can best come together to assist and make a difference. Serve as a resource and look for unique ways to strengthen and deepen your relationship. And don't forget to share stories and photos of your community involvement with your patients both on your website and in your office. Let them know what you are doing and why. Who knows? They may even choose to follow your example and become more involved in the community, too!

GIVE THANKS AND GIVE BACK

I am a big believer in giving—whether it be time, talents or financial resources. To me, it is a responsibility ... a part of community. So when medical practices ask me how they can better reach the communities they serve, I always recommend giving back to one or two local non-profits, often focused on healthcare, always with missions that inspire them. It could be an annual Thanksgiving or holiday "gift," or more of an ongoing commitment to volunteer or serve on a board of directors.

Once you have selected an organization to support, be creative. Involve your staff in brainstorming ideas to generate awareness and boost the impact of that gift. Make your contribution personal and memorable. Write a thoughtful note or letter to accompany your donation and have all of your staff sign it. Send a photo of your team showing their support (they could be holding signs or wearing buttons). Gather a couple team members to personally drop off the contribution. Create a memory for the receiving charity, and they, in turn, will remember you.

EXHIBIT 9.1 Texas Retina Associates Community Involvement— Event Program Ads

Texas Retina Associates in Dallas, Texas, identified several community organizations where their physicians and employee team had interests, ties or involvement. Here are a few program ads for events in which they have participated and supported.

REAL LIFE EXAMPLE

In 2009, after witnessing a steady stream of patients struggling after the economic downturn, Orlando ophthalmologist David B. Auerbach, DO, with Eye Physicians of Central Florida, decided he wanted to do something to give back and make a difference in his community. He was especially struck by the growing number of people suffering vision loss from cataracts who were unable to pay for the surgery because they were too young for Medicare and lacked the means to afford adequate health insurance. At about the same time, he read about a Texas ophthalmologist who performed free cataract surgeries every November. Thanksgiving had always been Dr. Auerbach's favorite holiday so to make it more meaningful for suffering cataract patients, he initiated his "Gift of Sight" program and reached out to the local medical community for additional support.

Dr. Auerbach began in May by sending out letters about his program to referring community optometrists so that they could help to begin identifying patients. He then conducted free screenings of potential patients to ensure they met the criteria for surgery. Dr. Auerbach also secured commitments from others whose support and in-kind contributions he needed to make his dream a reality—a local outpatient surgery center, anesthesiologist, and Alcon, the maker of the artificial lens that would be implanted.

Dr. Auerbach performed four surgeries that first year. All went well, and the patients were extremely gracious. It was a timely, heartwarming story that easily attracted the interest and attention of local media, resulting in several positive Thanksgiving news stories over the years of the program, including front page features in the major newspaper, on a local television station, in neighborhood magazines, and also in the *Orlando Medical News*, a publication for physicians and administrators within the local healthcare industry. See Exhibit 9.2 for a sample news release for the Gift of Sight program.

continued

EXHIBIT 9.2 Gift of Sight Program News Release

FOR IMMEDIATE RELEASE:

November 17, 2010

Media Contacts:

Andrea Eliscu

407-629-0062/mmiandrea@sprintmail.com

Debbie Muse, APR

407/484-1497/bdmuse@bellsouth.net

**Central Florida Doctor to Give the Gift of Sight
to Local Residents in Need**

ORLANDO, Fla. – David B. Auerbach, D.O., of Eye Physicians of Central Florida is holding his second annual "Gift of Sight" program this month, a Thanksgiving initiative that provides free cataract surgery to a select group of patients who lack insurance. He has reached out and identified four patients who are now scheduled for surgery on November 23, 2010.

"We continue to see and feel the negative impacts of the economy throughout our community," said Dr. Auerbach. "Personally, I am moved when I hear of people suffering vision loss from cataracts, yet they are unable to pay for the surgery because they are too young for Medicare or cannot afford health insurance. This is how our practice helps to make a difference and give back during these tough economic times. It is our Thanksgiving gift."

Once again, Dr. Auerbach has secured commitments from the Lake Mary Surgery Center, Alcon, anesthesiologist David Nussear, M.D., and operating room personnel who will donate their products and services to help make this year's effort possible.

One of the patients benefiting from this year's Gift of Sight program is 29-year-old Casselberry resident John Wilkinson. Wilkinson has suffered blindness in his left eye since age 15 due to a sports injury induced retinal detachment. However, he learned to adjust, maintain independence and continue on with his life. Until recently, he worked as a tree trimmer, and then about five months ago, began experiencing blurriness in his right eye which continued to worsen to the point of complete vision loss. He is now legally blind. This has caused him to lose his job and as a result, his home as well. A determined, hard-working and independent man, Wilkinson suddenly found himself completely dependent on the generosity and assistance of friends.

One of these friends, Jennifer Hicks, took Wilkinson in and also connected him with the Lion's Club who helped him secure an eye exam where it was determined that the blindness in his right eye was the result of a cataract that could be corrected with surgery. However, Wilkinson lacks health insurance and wasn't sure where to turn until he was connected with Dr. Auerbach's Gift of Sight program. Now he looks forward to regaining his sight in that eye along with his independence.

continued

EXHIBIT 9.2 Gift of Sight Program News Release

continued

"In the past few months, I have lost everything," said Wilkinson. "You have no idea what a blessing your sight is and how much it means to you until you lose it. I am so grateful to Dr. Auerbach and to my friends who have helped get me to my appointments. I can't wait to get back to work again – something safe and inside this time. I want to enjoy the simple things in life again – going for a walk, cooking, playing with my little girl. I also want to give back to all of those who have helped me through this."

Dr. Auerbach joined Eye Physicians of Central Florida in 2001 and specializes in general ophthalmology, refractive small-incision cataract surgery, neuro-ophthalmology and oculoplastic surgery. He earned his medical degree from the State University of New York at Stonybrook. Dr. Auerbach completed his residency in ophthalmology at the Philadelphia College of Osteopathic Medicine and his medical internship at Mount Clemens General Hospital. He also completed a fellowship in oculoplastic and reconstructive surgery at The Pavilions of Voorhees in New Jersey and a second fellowship in neuro-ophthalmology at Wills Eye Hospital in Philadelphia. An Osteopathic Fellow of the American Academy of Ophthalmology, Dr. Auerbach is certified by the American Osteopathic Board of Ophthalmology. He serves as a member of the North American Neuro-ophthalmic Society, the American Society of Cataract and Refractive Surgeons, the Florida Society of Ophthalmology and the Central Florida Society of Ophthalmology.

Established in 1981, Robert S. Gold, M.D., F.A.A.P., David B. Auerbach, D.O., Louis C. Blumenfeld, M.D., F.A.A.P., Victor B. Thomas, M.D., Jamie L. Ikeda, M.D., Lynda Z. Kleiman, M.D., and optometric physician Larry S. Lewis, O.D., of Eye Physicians of Central Florida care for children and adults of all ages, providing routine examinations, glasses, contact lenses, ophthalmic evaluation, treatment and surgery. They also specialize in pediatric ophthalmology, adult eye muscle disorders, cataract and laser surgery, neuro-ophthalmology, cornea and external disease, and oculoplastic, reconstructive and cosmetic eyelid surgery. The practice is a division of Florida Pediatric Associates, LLP, and accepts most major health insurance plans. For more information or to schedule an appointment, call 407-767-6411 or visit www.eyephy.com.

EVENTS

I talked a little about events when discussing engagement. Strategically participating in other organizations' events, where they make sense for your practice and target audience, can be an effective way to build awareness and relationships through positive community outreach. What about hosting your own event? Events require a financial and manpower investment with very little return unless done properly. As a result, I recommend that you be discerning in choosing an occasion to host an event. It could be a new office, a significant anniversary or the introduction of a new physician.

Although time is tight and schedules are increasingly overloaded, a properly executed, well-timed event (election years are great) can still build awareness and strengthen referral relationships for your practice. Here are a few keys to success:

1. **Basic invitations are not enough.** You need to go a step further. If you have the time and resources, a hand delivered invitation makes a stronger impression. Maybe someone from your staff could take a Friday afternoon to deliver the invitations along with a creative treat to your closest and most important invitees. Next comes follow up. Make a list of the top 20-40 people you really want at your event (i.e., top referring physician practices, friends of the practice, community leaders, etc.). Then have your physician(s) pick up the phone and call them with a personal follow-up invitation. Have several doctors in your group? Divvy up the list. Just about anyone can squeeze in five quick phone calls a day. Never underestimate the power of that personal outreach.

2. **Find a partner.** Hold your event in conjunction with another organization or business. This could be your local Chamber of Commerce or even other physician practices in your building or complex. Many Chambers, especially the smaller ones, will send their ambassadors out to do a ribbon cutting if it is a new office. Or perhaps see if they will let you host one of their monthly "Business After Hours" events. Either way, if you are a Chamber member, they will often help to promote your event to their membership (many of whom are well connected, looking for networking opportunities and will help generate buzz for you). Make the Chamber a part of your program, and you help establish your leadership presence within the business community.

3. **Invite local elected officials.** This is especially effective during election years. Ask them to help cut the ribbon if you are doing a ribbon cutting and be sure to give them a personal tour of your facility, including introductions to physicians, and staff members as well as explanations of key services and unique equipment or offerings.

4. **Invite local media.** While the major newspaper and TV stations probably won't find your event newsworthy, your local business journal and smaller community magazines or newspapers very well may. Some will at least send out a photographer or allow you to submit professional photos with captions after the event. If you do receive any media coverage,

be sure to highlight it on your own website and include links to stories and photos.

5. **Hire a professional photographer.** Make sure you find someone who has experience in covering events and will document who is in all photos. Then, after your event, send attendees photos featuring them along with a personal thank-you. You can do this electronically, by mail or through personal delivery. You can also post the photos on your website and social media (be sure to tag those you know).

6. **Don't forget the details**. One of the biggest keys to hosting a successful event is to "walk through" the event from a guest's perspective and think through every detail. Place outdoor way-finding yard signs with balloons attached. Designate parking areas (or better yet offer valet parking if parking is tight). If there is a good chance of rain, have umbrellas with your logo made and have them on hand to assist guests to and from their cars. Make sure your staff is dressed "in uniform" and prepared to greet guests and educate them about the practice. Give each guest a small thank-you gift on their way out (could be a creative promotional item printed with your logo, a small bag of custom cookies or candy, etc.)

7. **Don't forget entertainment.** No one likes a boring party. What can you do to add interest and make it more memorable? Entertainment doesn't have to cost a lot of money. Why not partner with a local school arts program or nonprofit organization? Many can offer small performing ensembles who are just as talented as the pros and would welcome the performance opportunity in return for a small donation to their program. Plus it shows goodwill to your local community. Or for a lighter event, set up a photo booth or hire a caricature artist. This is your chance to have some fun! Create memories!

I have seen several successful examples of effective events over the years. One large orthopedic practice I worked with in a smaller community held an annual summer block party to show appreciation for their colleagues and referral offices. It was something many in that community looked forward to each year.

Another practice I worked with, Eye Physicians of Central Florida, opened a new, larger, office custom-designed to better serve and meet the needs of eye care patients by improving **Access** and **Accommodation.** There was an outpatient surgery center downstairs, and they also shared the building with a children's ENT practice. When it came time to open the new building, all three entities combined forces to host an event for their referral sources, community business leaders, local elected officials and friends. Eye Physicians had joined the local Chamber of Commerce which held a ribbon cutting, helped market the event, coordinated local media relations and even provided a photographer to help document the event. Food and drink flowed throughout the building, tours were facilitated on each floor, and a local youth string ensemble provided entertainment on the first floor. The mayor attended along with local physicians and business leaders. It was a great success, a perfect introduction of the new facility to the community (many had watched the construction for months) and a memorable evening for all who attended.

ARE YOU A SATELLITE OR A NEIGHBORHOOD?

For many medical practices, opening another office is a great way to improve **Access** and **Availability**. Now you need to market it. While there are many creative and effective ways to do so, perhaps the most important boils down to one simple question:

What are you going to call it?

Too often, I hear the word "satellite," while the original or current office is referred to as the "main office." What message does this send to the new community you are trying to better serve? Are you circling above or are you establishing roots in the community?

How much better does it feel to go to a "neighborhood office" or a "community office?" Now I feel like you care about me—that you are a part of where I live and what I know.

No one wants to feel like an afterthought or second-rate citizen. Your patients want to feel like they are important no matter where they go to see you.

SUMMARY

The key to effective community relations is to find where you fit best and then become involved. However you decide to engage, make it sincere, make it genuine, make it creative, and it will be memorable. Done the right way, community involvement and outreach energizes, inspires, connects, propels and ripples out like a wave, touching people in places well beyond your immediate reach. It builds awareness and positively positions your practice as an involved leader. It will not only make your world a better place, it will expand it. So what are you waiting for?

DO THEY KNOW?

One of your physicians was just honored by the local homeless coalition for 10 years of service to the organization.

Another physician just completed his first marathon.

Your staff had the largest team at the diabetes walk last weekend.

These are all great ways your practice may be participating in your community, but do your patients know?

Start a blog on your website and update it with stories about your community relations activities. Post them on your social media, too. Frame a photo of your team in action out in the community and hang it on a wall in the office. Create a congratulations poster for the waiting room.

Your practice has a heart and soul. Be sure to share it with your patient family.

CHAPTER 10

Your Online Identity—
Websites and
Social Media

"Prosumers" turn to the web for almost every purchasing decision in their lives, and healthcare is no exception. Increasingly, healthcare costs are shifting from employers to individuals. Because consumers are paying more out of their own pockets, they are also spending more time scrutinizing their healthcare "purchasing" decisions.

Yes, patients want a qualified physician. But physicians, especially younger ones, are almost all board-certified and fellowship-trained. That has become an equalizer. So now a consumer is thinking if you and five other doctors in the community have the same training, what is it about you that makes you different and better? Is it your experience? Your outcomes? Your service? What are other patients saying about you? What do other physicians say about you?

Patients today still turn to friends, family, neighbors, co-workers and other physicians for referrals. However, in today's time-pressed, technology-driven world, the Web has become a second and in some cases, first "community" to turn to for this type of qualitative information.

A patient can go on Google and search for say, "orthopedic physician Orlando," and pull up websites for a number of physicians and practices. Based on the way they make other purchasing decisions, they expect your site to look modern, informative and easy to navigate. They also expect to see videos, blogs, testimonials and information not just on the physicians' training but also on what makes them stand out and how other patients feel about the care they have received.

Prosumers also welcome and value the feedback of social communities.

Bottom line—your website and social media presence have become key parts of your "word of mouth" or as some now call it "world of mouth."

BASIC BUILDING BLOCKS OF AN EFFECTIVE WEBSITE

Your website truly is an extension of you and your practice. Think of it as another way to enhance the experience you provide to your customers—patients, family members and referral sources alike. Here are a few basic building blocks:

1. **Performance and Functionality**—This means that your site does what it should whenever it is accessed or needed. It loads quickly and correctly. All buttons, tabs and links throughout the site work properly. Any online forms are error-free and easy to use. And the site performs well on search engines.

2. **Organization and Navigation**—Those visiting your site want it to meet their needs quickly. That means you need to position the most important information on the top half of the page, including your phone number and address. Your website visitors also must be able to easily navigate and find what they want. Key tabs/pages for most medical practices include:

   ○ About Us

   ○ Physicians/Providers

   ○ Services

   ○ Locations

   ○ Contact Us

   ○ Patient Resource

   ○ News

   Some sites also include a separate tab/page just for referring physicians.

3. **Design**—Keep the design of your site simple and clean; you want to be sure it loads quickly. This doesn't mean the design can't be creative and compelling. A good web firm will help you to reach the right balance. I also recommend that you avoid "template" sites. If the goal of your

branding is to deliver a healthcare experience for your patients that is specific and unique to your practice, using a template to build your website—one that looks like numerous other medical practices—is simply not an effective approach.

4. **Content**—The most important element of any website is the content. Make sure it is clear, concise and useful. It can't be *Gone with the Wind*. Put yourself in the shoes of a patient or caregiver. What information do you most want to know? What additional information will help to guide your health journey? Consider formatting your content in brief copy blocks with lots of headings and sub-headings as well as bullet points and lists to make it easy to find, reference, read and digest.

5. **Mobile-friendly**—Your patients are increasingly dependent on their smartphones and tablets for the information they need to guide their lives. As a result, your website must be mobile friendly. In addition, as of April 2015, Google now uses "mobile-friendliness" as a key factor in its search engine rankings (more on that later). Google offers a simple tool to see if your current site fits the mobile-friendly bill https://www.google.com/webmasters/tools/mobile-friendly/.

6. **Frequent Updates**—Your website should be maintained and updated frequently. This means not only keeping contact information like addresses, phone numbers and office hours current, but also adding new physicians, locations or services in a timely manner. It also means deleting anything that is no longer relevant (i.e., physicians who have retired or left, insurance plans no longer covered, etc.). I also encourage practices to work with their web firm to track, report and adjust the site as needed for optimal performance.

Here are a few strong medical websites you may wish to browse:

- www.jlrmedicalgroup.com
- www.centerforpain.com
- www.neurospineinstitute.com
- www.jewettortho.com

THE DANGER OF ONLINE FORMS
AND THE NEED FOR A TEST DRIVE

Offering online forms on your website is a beautiful thing. Done correctly, they improve **Access** and increase your **Availability** and **Accommodation** of your patients. Too often, however, practices put the forms "on the lot" before taking them for a test drive.

No doubt you've experienced it at some point, if not with a medical practice, then in some sort of online transaction. You click on the link for an online form only to find it doesn't work, the directions aren't clear, or it won't allow you to enter the full information that is requested. You end up confused or frustrated and have to pick up the phone to call for assistance or worse yet, you just give up. I suspect the person who created or uploaded the form never tested it on real end users. And in today's world of pay-for-performance, patient satisfaction (yes, even the experience of completing forms) is more critical than ever before.

Your online forms should be as simple, clear and user-friendly as possible. This means easy-to-understand directions, a logical flow and the avoidance of redundant information requests when at all possible. Have a few folks from outside your office take your forms for a spin—people who are looking at it from an end-user perspective rather than someone who needs the information. It will be well worth the extra step.

FINDING THE RIGHT WEB PARTNER/QUESTIONS TO ASK WHEN INTERVIEWING FIRMS

My number one recommendation for building a successful website is to hire a professional. This is one of the most important tools for marketing your practice and as a result no place for an amateur. I realize many physicians and administrators balk at the upfront cost, but I promise you the investment will be well worth it in the long run.

Hiring a professional, however, does not mean that you are off the hook. Building an effective website is a team project, and it starts with a little homework on your end:

1. Identify a point person for the project. You need to designate a single, senior-level person within your practice who will be responsible for working with the design firm and coordinating internal input/feedback.

2. Compile a list of your competitors and their web addresses.

3. Identify three to five websites you like (either in your specialty or not) and provide a brief explanation of why you like each one. Even better, also find three you don't like and explain why. This will help your design firm better understand what you want.

4. Write out your goals for creating the new site. What is most important? What are the key messages? What do you hope to achieve?

5. Determine your budget.

6. Define your target audience(s). Provide as much of a detailed description as possible.

You can then compile all of this great information into a background document to share with potential web firms.

Now that you've done your homework, you need to identify at least three qualified web development firms and secure comprehensive proposals from each. Where to start? Talk to your colleagues and other healthcare leaders in your community to secure recommendations of firms to pursue. Then look at the firms' websites and review samples of their past work. Most also list or include current or past clients on their websites. Talk to those clients and get additional feedback.

As you are interviewing potential web firms, here are some questions to ask:

1. Do you have any areas/industries of specialty?

2. Do you have any experience building healthcare/medical sites?

3. What is your typical timeframe for development of a new site?

4. Will the site be built from scratch or from a template design?

5. Who writes the content?

6. What do you expect us (the client) to provide?

7. Will the site have a content management system (CMS) so that we can easily make changes and updates after it is built and live? How do you handle more significant changes/updates (that can't be handled by a CMS) down the road? What is that process and fee?

8. What level of ongoing support do you provide? What is the fee for that support and basic site maintenance?

9. Do you have a minimum charge for a new site design?

10. Do you provide your clients with any metrics or tracking of site performance? If so, how often and in what format? Do you recommend changes based on those results? Is this standard or an extra charge? If extra, how much?

11. Do you have experience with search engine optimization (SEO), including ad words and pay per click (PPC) campaigns? How will you optimize the site?

12. How do you select and secure photography and images for the site?

13. When building a new site, how many initial design concepts will you provide us?

14. Do you have experience with online videos (i.e., bios and testimonials)? Do you have capabilities in-house to produce these or is there someone you contract with or can recommend to assist with this?

15. How will the website integrate with our social media sites (if the practice uses them)?

16. Will you test the site prior to launch to make sure it works on all of the major web browsers?

Once you have received the proposals, take your time reviewing them. Be sure you are comparing apples to apples, and don't be afraid to ask about anything that looks different or appears to be missing. Finally, here are a few pitfalls to avoid in making your final selection:

1. **Choosing based on price alone.** I realize budgets are tight, and cost is a key consideration. However, choosing the cheapest firm is typically not the best decision.

2. **Contracting a non-full-time professional to build the website.** It seems everyone knows someone who can build a website "on the side" (i.e., it is not their primary job). Be wary of this type of arrangement. Someone who is working on your site "part time" may not be able to complete it in a timely manner and also may not be around later to provide maintenance or support should you run into any issues or need changes. In addition, it is rare to find an individual who is an expert in all aspects of web design, including programming, content and design. That is why most firms typically have a team of professionals who pool their talents to build your site.

3. **Not having a point person for the project.** I can't emphasize enough how important it is to have a point person within your organization who is accountable and will make sure information is gathered, deadlines are met, reviews/approvals are made, and ultimately, the site gets done.

SHARE YOUR STORY

We're all familiar with the traditional physician website bio that reads like a CV—medical school, internship, residency and fellowship. Some are written in prose while others are bulleted out by category. While this information is important and needs to be there, the problem is that even with stellar training and credentials, these types of bios all start to look the same. What your potential patients and referring physicians really want to know is who you are and what makes you different. This means you need to share your story:

- Why did you go into medicine?

- Why did you choose your specialty?

- What do you enjoy most about your work?

- What inspires you?

- What do you do outside of work that is interesting?

- How do you give back to the community?

- What legacy do you hope to leave in your practice? in your field? to the world?

These are just a few questions to help get you started. Whether you share your story in a brief video bio (my preference) or in written form on your website, do share it. You will be amazed at how it attracts interest, forges connections and strengthens bonds.

OPTIMIZE FOR SUCCESSFUL SEARCHES

According to a study conducted by Google, 84 percent of consumers use search engines to gather information for local purchases, and healthcare is a local purchasing decision. Website optimization is also known as search engine optimization (SEO), and involves a number of back-end strategies in the construction of your site, such as keywords and meta tags, that help to increase its rankings in search engines such as Google or Bing. Optimization helps to increase visits to your site and more importantly, when done correctly, helps to ensure those visitors match your desired target market. The goal is to enhance **Accessibility** so that people find you when they need you most. A good web firm can help you to not only build a site that meets the needs of your current customers but also one that will perform well with search engines to attract new customers to your practice.

One final thought on optimization that I mentioned earlier in this chapter, but that bears repeating: Make sure you have a mobile-friendly site. As of April 2015, Google now "punishes" sites that do not meet this criterion. This means that having a site that is not optimized for use on mobile devices can lower your Google search ranking--you may not even appear on the first page of search results. So, be sure your site fits the bill.

A MOVIE IS WORTH A THOUSAND WORDS— INCORPORATING VIDEO IN YOUR WEBSITE

I am a big believer in the power of video on a website, and here are some figures that help explain why:

- According to comScore, 87% of American internet users watch online videos, and 92% of mobile viewers share online videos with friends and families.

- According to Hubspot, 78% of people watch videos online every week, and 55% every day.

- Hubspot also reports that 65% of video viewers watch more than 3/4 of a video.

- According to Adelie Studios, the average internet user spends 88% more time on a website with video than without, and 64% of consumers are more likely to buy a product after watching a video about it.

- Diode Digital found that 60% of website visitors will watch a video before reading any text.

In fact, numerous studies have shown that more than any other type of web content, video marketing converts to "traffic" and "leads," which means more people coming to your site and ultimately, more patients and customers attracted to your practice. Here are two of the most powerful ways to use online video for your medical practice:

1. **Physician Bios/Profiles**—These let prospective patients see you as a human being and not just a thumbnail photo with a medical resume. One of the most successful ways to do video profiles so that they come across more natural and less "rehearsed" is to use an interview format where someone asks the physician questions, and then the physician answers in an improvised, unscripted manner. You can edit out the interviewer and either replace with a graphic of the question or encourage the physician to repeat the question or work it into the response.

2. **Patient Stories/Testimonials**—This is a powerful way to leverage your greatest asset: satisfied patients. Again, an interview style works well so that the video feels natural and conversational. The whole idea is to let patients tell their "stories" and experiences with your practice and physicians in their own words. It can be a dramatic, "life-changing" story like regaining movement or vision, or it can simply be a story about how a physician went above and beyond in providing care or service to make a difference in someone's life. Some of these videos use a narrator to help with connection and flow while others don't. Both can work. For some good examples, check out: http://neurospineinstitute.org/company/patient-testimonials.

For both physician bios and patient testimonials, try to keep the video to between two and five minutes. In addition, encourage viewers to share the video with others by providing a "share" button for both e-mail and the primary social media sites like Facebook, Twitter and LinkedIn. This not only boosts your social media presence (more on that later), it provides a great resource to patients and caregivers who want to share information about their physicians with family members or friends.

Once you get your feet wet with physician bio and patient testimonial videos, you can then consider incorporating additional online videos, including health minutes and patient education just to name a few. For some good examples, check out Jewett Orthopedic Clinic's You Tube channel JewettOrtho: www.you-tube.com/user/JewettOrtho.

IN OTHERS' WORDS—PROTECT YOURSELF WHEN USING THE POWER OF TESTIMONIALS

While testimonials and endorsements can be powerful online tools, be careful to stay within Federal Trade Commission (FTC) guidelines. Here are a few simple rules and recommendations to follow:

1. Don't hire paid endorsers.

2. Only feature actual patients.

3. Be sure to have patients who provide testimonials sign a legally binding authorization form. Your attorney should be able to assist you in crafting one.

4. Have patients share their stories in their own words. Don't provide them with a script. Instead, interview them, asking questions they can answer.

5. Be honest and open—clearly identify the physician by name and avoid partial disclosure or misrepresentation of facts.

6. Don't compensate patients in any way for their testimonial.

I also encourage you to check and abide by any additional rules from your State Board of Medicine, HIPAA and your own professional liability policy.

Testimonials and endorsements can be invaluable marketing for your practice. Just be sure to cover your bases.

MEETING PATIENTS' NEEDS—INCREASING ACCESS THROUGH PORTALS

Another online tool—the patient portal—is a perfect example of **The 4 A's— Access, Availability, Accommodation** and **Accountability**—in action. This secure, online site gives your patients convenient, 24-hour access to both your practice and their personal health information. Logging in using a secure username and password, patients can view health information such as:

- Lab results
- Imaging reports
- Recent doctor visit or discharge summaries
- Medications
- Immunizations
- Allergies

Some patient portals also allow patients to:

- Request prescription refills
- Download and complete forms
- Communicate via secure e-mail with their healthcare provider
- Schedule non-urgent appointments
- Make payments
- Check benefits and coverage
- Update contact information
- View educational materials

If you have a patient portal, it should seamlessly integrate and be easily accessible within your website. It is a great way to improve patient care and outcomes by enhancing communication between your patients and providers, expanding your **Access** and **Availability**, **Accommodating** and empowering your patients and providing **Accountability** and service in between patient visits.

KEEPING IT FRESH—CONTENT IS KING

So you've built a great new website. It's easy to push that project aside and shift your focus to something else. However, the key to an effective website is keeping it fresh with new content. This means more than just staying current with the most accurate information like office hours and phone numbers. It means creating brand new content as well. One of the easiest ways to do this is to start a blog on your site where you can post brief updates on practice news and timely health topics. Think of a blog as your voice in the medical community.

This isn't nearly as daunting as it may sound. There are exciting things going on within your practice every week. You may be so busy that you just don't notice them. You should encourage your staff to share these updates with you when they occur.

Did one of your staff members celebrate a significant service anniversary with the practice?

Did anyone on your team participate in a community event or receive an award?

Are there seasonal office reminders you need to promote and share like flu shots or back-to-school physicals?

You can also provide your take on healthcare issues in the news, the latest research in your field, new medications or treatments on the market, new health guidelines or recommendations, or even healthy living tips. For example, the Zika virus is in the news. One of our OB/GYN clients has talked about this in his blog, educating his patients on what they need to know, confronting the myths and highlighting the facts.

Content helps to:

- Maximize your website's performance.
- Increase your exposure and awareness in the community.
- Improve patient satisfaction.
- Position you as an expert in your field.

We've all heard the excuse, "I don't have time." There are a number of ways to fit blog posts into a busy schedule:

1. Set a goal of one article a month.

2. Work ahead. Knock out several articles at one time that can be used throughout the year. These can be evergreen or seasonal in nature. For example, if you have an ophthalmology practice, you could focus on eye strain during the back-to-school time period, eye allergies in the spring when the pollen peaks, and eye safety or sun protection in the summer as everyone is headed outdoors.

3. Hire someone to ghostwrite posts for you and then edit them, adding your personal take or touch.

Make content a priority and use it well. You will be pleasantly surprised at what it can do for you.

SOCIAL MEDIA—PLAN, COMMIT, INVITE, ENGAGE, EVALUATE

Social media is everywhere. For healthcare organizations, using it can be a great tactic to help build and strengthen your base. However, like any tactic, it comes with its own set of unique challenges and if not handled properly, it can turn into wasted resources or even backfire on you.

So many people and businesses jump into social media because it is the latest "thing." That should not be a reason to do it. There are, however, many valid reasons:

* Are you trying to increase overall brand awareness?

* Do you want to build or strengthen loyalty/retention with current patients and customers?

* Are you trying to generate buzz about something new?

* Do you have a product or service you want to sell?

* Are you trying to cross-market services to your existing customer base?

Your reason(s) will dictate how you engage and what you say. Before moving forward with a social media strategy, I recommend a four-step process:

1. **Plan**—Like any new marketing vehicle, you need to think through how social media will fit into your overall marketing plan before you dive right in. This means it should be just one tactic of many. What are your practice goals and priorities? Who are you trying to reach? What will you communicate/share? Who will initiate and manage your posts? Does this person have access and enough time to effectively manage your social media? Can you respond to comments in a timely and appropriate manner? The power of social media is in its ability to spark and engage in conversation, to build interest and loyalty at a grassroots level. Set realistic goals and timelines for what you hope to achieve. And don't forget to determine how you are going to define and measure success.

2. **Commit**—Don't start what you can't finish. Too many businesses (not just healthcare) jump into social media, initially investing great amounts of energy and resources, and then once they realize the ongoing commit-

ment of time and energy required, they fizzle out. If you are going to do social media, ensure you have someone on your team who is accountable and committed to making it work for your practice long term.

3. **Invite**—Just because you build it does not mean they will come. To be successful with social media, you need to invite participation. Find ways within your practice to let your patients know about your social media presence and encourage them to engage. You can e-mail an invitation with links to your social media sites as well as post signs or flyers in your waiting and patient exam rooms, letting folks know. Empower your staff to inform patients, especially at check-in or check-out. And promote your website and social media sites on all of your printed and electronic marketing materials/communication.

4. **Engage**—Don't simply be a loudspeaker. Sharing all of that great content you have created is wonderful. However, if you only use social media to "push out" your own message, you are not only missing the point of this tool, you will quickly lose followers. Yes, you can give updates and share news (having that blog and posting links to new posts is a great way to feed your followers), but also be sure to ask questions and start conversations. Ask your followers what they think about something. Find out what they feel, value and want to know about your practice or specialty. Get them talking about you. And be sure to listen, acknowledge their input and deliver the information they want. Just be careful to abide by patient privacy rules and avoid providing medical advice/treatment online.

For a great example of a medical practice successfully using social media, check out Jewett Orthopedic Clinic on Facebook.

Social media can be an effective way to enhance your marketing. However, like so many things in life and business, you will only get out of it what you put into it.

SOCIAL MEDIA: LOUDSPEAKER VS. GRAPEVINE

It's easy to tell your own story. You know it by heart. However, it's much more powerful and effective to let others do it for you. That has always been the power of public relations, and it is one of the true gems of social media. Think of it as the loudspeaker vs. the grapevine. Which do you pay attention and listen to? Which holds more credibility? Make sure your social media videos and messages aren't just about sharing your message (the loudspeaker). Get the grapevine going. Invite your patients to share their personal experiences with your practice. Initially, it may take a bit more time and effort engaging "followers," but the results will be well worth the positive world of mouth in the end.

CHAPTER 11

When Change Happens

Change. Almost no one likes it. Yet, it is inevitable, especially in today's rapidly evolving world of healthcare. A physician joins your group, a physician leaves your group, a physician retires, you close an office, you open an office, you merge with another group, you're stuck in negotiations with a health plan. As much as these changes can stress and even frustrate you, try to take a step back and imagine how they make your patients feel.

Don't get so caught up in the internal details and challenges that you miss the opportunity to demonstrate to your patients how much you truly care. When change happens, communicate early and often—whether in person, a written letter, e-mail, phone call, signage, your website, Facebook, Twitter or perhaps even all of the above. Explain the change, why it is happening and how you are going to do everything in your power to minimize its impact on them. Acknowledge. Assure. Answer. Accommodate. Assist. That is how you build and strengthen relationships in times of stress. That is how you stand out from the "system."

In this chapter, I will touch on some of the most common changes and share some real-life examples of how other medical practices have handled them.

PHYSICIAN RETIRING/LEAVING THE PRACTICE

This is one of the toughest changes to deal with. Not only are you losing a colleague or partner, patients, especially those who have been with your practice for many years, become attached to "their" physician and feel a true loss when they leave. Your job is to acknowledge this loss and help to quickly and smoothly transition them to another physician (hopefully within your practice) who can meet their needs. And the key to doing this successfully is communication, communication, communication:

1. **Inform staff first.** As with any change, make sure your staff understands early on what will happen and that they have the information they need to assist patients with questions or concerns during the transition.

2. **Send a letter to patients.** Send a personal letter to each of the physician's patients. Keep it warm and conversational. Detail how the transition will take place and provide them with contact information should they have any questions. If the parting is on good terms and time allows, it is best to have this letter come from the physician who is leaving. If not, it can come from another senior physician or administrator in the practice. See Exhibits 11.1 - 11.3 for some examples.

3. **Don't forget one-on-one communication.** Don't rely completely on the patient letter mailing. Once the announcement has been made, reinforce and reassure patients affected by the change while they are there in your office. The physician leaving can take the opportunity to say good-bye in person and if possible, introduce them to the physician(s) who will be taking over their patients' care. If a personal introduction is not possible, the physician retiring or leaving can at least talk about the new/other physician(s)—his or her background, qualifications and how they trust that physician(s) to care for their patients.

4. **Send a letter to referring physicians and "friends" of the practice.** No one likes to hear news through the grapevine. As you are sending a letter to patients, send a variation of that letter to referring physicians and others (i.e., hospital staff, key vendors, etc.) who should know about the change. Express appreciation for their trust and referrals, inform them about timing and the transition, and let them know about other physicians within your practice who are available to care for their patients.

5. **Update your website and social media.** In addition to keeping the information current, add a news story about the change and include links to it in posts on your social media sites. Also, if there is a transition period, add a banner, note or update to your home page and/or that physician's bio page, letting patients know about the change. The content should be an abbreviated form of what you shared in the patient letter.

6. **Place a legal ad in the local newspaper.** If you have a physician retiring, check with your attorney to see if by law you are required to post this sort of public notice. Exhibit 11.4 has an example of messaging.

EXHIBIT 11.1 Physician Retirement Letter to Patients

Dear PATIENT NAME:

It is with great appreciation and much sadness that we announce the retirement, effective immediately, of Dr. Snyder from our practice due to health issues.

I know I speak on his behalf when I say it has been his true privilege and honor to care for you. Dr. Snyder was a founder of our practice and has served patients like you and thousands of others throughout our community for more than 40 years now. His dedication to each individual patient, his commitment to our community, and his medical leadership helped lay the foundation for our practice and continue to serve as an inspiration to us all.

We know this news has come suddenly, and we want to assure you that Texas Retina Associates remains committed to meeting your needs. All of Dr. Snyder's current appointments are being transitioned to our other physicians in the Dallas and Paris offices, including Drs. Vaiser, Fuller, Fish, Spencer, Anand, Wang, Coors and Csaky in Dallas, and Drs. Spencer and Csaky in Paris.

We are doing everything we can to ensure a seamless transition so you won't experience any care, coverage or claims issues. As always, our physicians and staff will continue to work together to provide you the best possible vitreoretinal care in the office you know. And our team is here to answer any questions or address any concerns you may have so please don't hesitate to call us.

Sincerely,
Senior Physician, MD

EXHIBIT 11.2 Sample Physician Leaving/Moving Letter

Dear PATIENT NAME:

Thank you for privilege of caring for your eyes. I am writing to you on behalf of myself, Dr. Michel Shami and the staff of Texas Retina Associates in Lubbock. I wanted to let you know that for personal reasons I have decided to move from the Lubbock area. I will be discontinuing my practice as of December 31, 2010.

I want to assure you that Texas Retina Associates remains committed to meeting your needs and will do everything to accommodate you and ensure a seamless transition so you won't experience any care, coverage or claims issues. My partners and staff know and care about you, and will continue to work together to provide you the best possible vitreoretinal care in the same office location. Dr. Shami will continue to serve the Lubbock office and in January, will be joined by Sushma Vance, MD.

Dr. Vance has completed her retina fellowship with Manhattan Eye, Ear, and Throat Hospital, Vitreous-Retina Macula Consultants of New York and Texas Retina Associates in Dallas. She completed her residency, internship and medical degree at Northeastern Ohio Universities College of Medicine. Dr. Vance is a member of the American Academy of Ophthalmology and the Association for Research in Vision and Ophthalmology (ARVO).

I have every confidence that Dr. Vance will provide you with excellent care. She is well known to the physicians of Texas Retina Associates through her fellowship. Not only does she have stellar credentials, she shares our philosophy of providing you with personal, attentive and professional care. She will certainly enhance the level of care we are able to provide patients throughout the Lubbock community.

As always, the staff in the Lubbock office are here to answer any questions you may have. It has truly been an honor and privilege to serve you. I wish you the best of luck and continued health.

Sincerely,

Stephen Smith, MD

EXHIBIT 11.3 Sample Physician Moving/Leaving Letter

Dear Patients and Friends:

I wanted to reach out and personally let you know that I am moving my practice to Physician Associates' Baldwin Park office full-time as of April 1. I appreciate the trust you have placed in me and am happy to see you in my new location. However, I certainly understand if you prefer to stay with the West Orlando/Ocoee office. To that end, I am pleased to introduce you to Hector F. Ramirez, MD, FACOG, an experienced and board-certified OB/GYN, who will begin seeing patients in the West Orlando/Ocoee office on April 1.

Fluent in both English and Spanish, Dr. Ramirez specializes in minimally invasive surgery and also completed extensive training in high-risk obstetrics. He provides a full range of women's healthcare services, including annual well-woman exams, pregnancy care and gynecological care.

Dr. Ramirez earned his medical degree from Ponce School of Medicine in Ponce, Puerto Rico, and completed his residency at Orlando Regional Healthcare. He is a diplomate of the American Board of Obstetrics and Gynecology and a fellow of the American Congress of Obstetricians and Gynecologists. A West Orange resident himself, he is looking forward to serving the community he calls home.

Please join me in extending Dr. Ramirez a warm welcome. To schedule your next appointment with him, please call 407.306.6386. Or if you prefer to see me in the Baldwin Park office, please call 407.898.6588.

We look forward to seeing you soon!

Cordially,

Pranav Chudgar, MD

EXHIBIT 11.4 Newspaper Legal Notice Ad

Notice to Patients

Robert S. Iurcovich, MD
1811 Lucerne Terrace
Orlando, FL 32806

The physicians and staff of Orlando Health Physician Associates would like to wish Robert S. Iurcovich, MD, all the best in his retirement and thank him for his many years of dedicated service to this community. Dr. Iurcovich's retirement was effective December 31, 2015, and that office is now closed.

Orlando Health Physician Associates will work with Dr. Iurcovich's patients to ensure a seamless transition of care to one of our other physicians. Patient medical records will remain on file with Orlando Health Physician Associates unless otherwise notified.

To schedule an appointment with one of our other physicians
or for questions about your records, please call

407-389-5332

NEW PHYSICIAN JOINING YOUR PRACTICE

A new physician joining your practice is a great opportunity to reach out and reconnect with your patients, referring physicians and community at large to share the good news. As with any communication effort, plan and work ahead to ensure all of the critical pieces are executed at the right time. Once you have officially made the hire, be sure to secure the new physician's latest CV and bio as well as a professional, high-resolution head shot photo. You will need these to develop key communication pieces before he or she arrives, which include:

1. **Website and Social Media**—Be sure to add the new physician to your website in all of the appropriate places, including creating his or her bio page. You can also create a news story announcing the physician's arrival, and if you are using social media, you can share a link to this article with your followers.

2. **Poster and/or Flyers**—Create a poster welcoming the new physician that can be mounted on an easel and placed in your waiting room to help inform patients. See Exhibit 11.5 for an example. Just keep the content concise so it

is visually appealing and easy to read. You can also consider creating a complementary flyer with more detail about the new physician to place on tables in your waiting and exam rooms.

3. **Announcement Card**—Create an announcement card that can be mailed to your referring physicians. See Exhibit 3.6 in Chapter 3 for an example.

4. **Patient Letter**—Craft a personal letter to patients, welcoming the new physician, and sharing his or her background and credentials. Don't be afraid to ask for referrals of their friends and family. See Exhibits 11.6 and 11.7 for sample letters.

5. **Business Cards and Bio Cards**—Be sure the new physician has new business cards ready to go the day he or she arrives. These will be critical as the physician begins networking and developing referral relationships as discussed in Chapter 3. Many of the practices I work with also develop rack-size bio cards for each of their physicians to use as a leave behind when making referral visits or talks in the community. Exhibits 11.8 and 11.9 provide two different examples.

6. **News Release**—Having a new physician join your practice is a great opportunity to send a news release to local publications in your market. Many, especially business journals, even have a special section dedicated to new professionals in the community. I have included a sample news release in Exhibit 11.10.

EXHIBIT 11.5 New Physician Poster

PHYSICIAN ASSOCIATES

ORLANDO HEALTH

WELCOME TO THE FAMILY!

Ana Castoro, MD
Family Medicine

"Since I was a child, I have had a passion for helping people. I love family medicine because it allows me to care for people in all stages of life — from children to the elderly. I believe in taking the time to help my patients understand and manage their current health problems as well as learn how to prevent new ones."

Certification: Board-certified in Family Medicine
Medical Education: University of Illinois at Chicago College of Medicine
Residency: Mayo Clinic School of Graduate Medical Education

Fluent in English and Spanish   550 East State Road 434
                                                                      Longwood, FL 32750

Dr. Castoro is currently accepting new patients.   407.381.7367

www.paof.com

EXHIBIT 11.6 New Physician Patient Letter

Dear Patients and Friends:

As you know, Dr. Gerkovich recently retired from practice after serving the Baldwin Park community for many years. We are happy to announce that one of our experienced women's health physicians, Pranav Chudgar, MD, has joined our Baldwin Park office and is currently accepting new patients.

Dr. Chudgar was born in New York and grew up in Augusta, Georgia. He and his family live in Baldwin Park so he is looking forward to serving the neighborhood he calls home. Most recently, he has been serving patients in our West Orlando office in Ocoee.

After earning his medical degree from the Medical College of Georgia, Dr. Chudgar completed his residency right here in Orlando at Winnie Palmer Hospital where he served as Chief Resident and earned an Exemplary Physician Award as well as a Physician Excellence Award in Obstetrics/Gynecology.

With Dr. Danna and Dr. Chudgar, we will continue to provide our Baldwin Park patients a full range of women's healthcare services, including annual well-woman exams, pregnancy care, gynecological care, and minimally invasive surgery.

Dr. Chudgar's current patients absolutely love him, and we know you will, too. To schedule your next appointment, please call 407.898.6588. We look forward to seeing you soon!

Warmly,

Dennis Buhring
President

EXHIBIT 11.7 New Physician Assistant Patient Letter

Dear Patients and Friends:

It is my pleasure to welcome Amara Travers, PA, our new Physician Assistant to the practice.

Amara is excited to joins us as Orlando is her hometown community. Like me, Amara is passionate about promoting heath and helping others, and we will work closely together to care for our patients.

Amara graduated from Barry University's Physician Assistant program in 2014, and is nationally certified and licensed in the state of Florida. In addition, she has participated in multiple medical missions, all the way from Swaziland, Africa, to the Amazon River in Brazil.

Please join me in extending Amara a warm welcome. She has openings in her schedule for new patients and would welcome referrals of your family, friends and neighbors. To schedule your next appointment with her, please call 407-985-1670.

Warmly,

Michael Young, MD

EXHIBIT 11.8 Sample Rack Card - Abbey *FRONT*

ASHKAN M. ABBEY, MD
VITREORETINAL SPECIALIST

Fellowship:	**Vitreoretinal Surgery** **William Beaumont Hospital,** **Associated Retinal Consultants** Royal Oak, Michigan
Residency:	**Ophthalmology** **University of Miami, Bascom Palmer Eye Institute** Miami, Florida
Internship:	**Scripps Mercy Hospital** San Diego, California
Medical School:	**Weill Cornell Medical College,** *with Honors* New York, New York
College:	**Harvard College,** *Magna Cum Laude* Cambridge, Massachusetts
Certification:	**American Board of Ophthalmology**
Academic Appointment:	**UT Southwestern Medical Center** Clinical Assistant Professor of Ophthalmology
Professional Affiliations:	American Academy of Ophthalmology, *Fellow* American Society of Retina Specialists Association for Research in Vision and Ophthalmology Alpha Omega Alpha Honor Medical Society *RETINA: The Journal of Retina and Vitreous* *Diseases,* Manuscript Referee
Research:	Published numerous peer-reviewed scientific papers, book chapters and national meeting abstracts
Clinical Expertise:	Diagnosis and treatment of macular degeneration, retinal detachment, diabetic retinopathy, macular holes, retinopathy of prematurity, and other pediatric retinal diseases

WWW.TEXASRETINA.COM

EXHIBIT 11.8 Sample Rack Card - Abbey   *BACK*

OFFICE LOCATIONS:

DALLAS MAIN
9600 N. Central Expressway
Suite 100
Dallas, Texas 75231
214-692-6941
214-739-5797 fax

ROCKWALL
2380 S. Goliad Street
Suite 120
Rockwall, Texas 75032
972-722-4739
972-722-4807 fax

Established more than 50 years ago, Texas Retina Associates, now with 14 offices throughout the state, is Texas' largest, most experienced ophthalmology practice focused specifically on the diagnosis, treatment and surgery of the retina and vitreous. We believe in providing personal, attentive, professional and convenient care as well as access to the latest technology and treatments. **Learn more about us at www.texasretina.com.**

EXHIBIT 11.9 Sample Rack Card - Laruidsen *FRONT*

PHYSICIAN ASSOCIATES

ORLANDO HEALTH

MEET

Deborah Lauridsen, MD
Family Medicine

7408 Red Bug Lake Road
Oviedo, FL 32765

407.381.7387

Your Partner on the Journey to Optimum Health

www.paof.com

EXHIBIT 11.9 Sample Rack Card - Laruidsen   BACK

Your Partner on the Journey to Optimum Health

Deborah Lauridsen, MD
Family Medicine

"From a very young age, I knew I wanted to be a doctor, and I continue to learn from my patients every day. I am passionate about helping them transition from sickness to health and believe that when people are given knowledge about their health, they have the power to be in control of their lives."

Certification: Board-certified in Family Medicine
Medical Education: Ross University School of Medicine
Residency: Northside Medical Center, Youngstown, Ohio

Fluent in English and Spanish

Services:
- Annual physicals
- School and sports physicals
- Vaccinations, including flu shots
- Care for common illnesses
- Management of chronic diseases like diabetes
- Preventive health care

Warmly welcoming new patients!

PHYSICIAN ASSOCIATES

ORLANDO HEALTH
7408 Red Bug Lake Road
Oviedo, FL 32765

407.381.7387

WELCOME!

www.paof.com

EXHIBIT 11.10 New Physician News Release

FOR IMMEDIATE RELEASE:

January 11, 2016

Media Contacts:

Jeff Brockette

214-692-6941/jbrockette@texasretina.com

Fran Crawford

214-692-6941/fcrawford@texasretina.com

Texas Retina Associates Welcomes Vitreoretinal Specialist

Christopher G. Fuller, MD

Lubbock, Tex.—Texas Retina Associates welcomes board-certified ophthalmologist and retina specialist Christopher G. Fuller, MD, to its Lubbock office starting January 11, 2016.

Born, raised and trained in Texas, Dr. Fuller has more than six years of experience as a vitreoretinal surgeon. He is fluent in Spanish and welcomes Spanish-speaking patients. Dr. Fuller provides diagnosis, treatment and surgery for disorders of the retina and vitreous, including retinal tears and detachments, age-related macular degeneration, diabetes, and macular holes and membranes. He completed his fellowship at Texas Retina Associates in 2009, and went on to serve as a vitreoretinal surgeon in Santa Fe, New Mexico, and then Houston, Texas, before returning to Texas Retina Associates. Dr. Fuller completed his residency at the University of Texas at Southwestern Medical Center in Dallas, and his internship at Texas A&M Scott & White Hospital in Temple. He earned his medical degree from Texas Tech University Health Sciences Center in Lubbock, and serves as a member of the American Academy of Ophthalmology, the American Society of Retina Specialists, Texas Medical Association, and the Lubbock-Crosby-Garza County Medical Society.

"We have known Dr. Fuller for a long time as his father, Dwain G. Fuller, MD, has been a leader in our practice for more than 35 years," said Texas Retina Associates CEO Jeff Brockette. "The Lubbock community continues to grow, and we are thrilled Dr. Fuller has decided to come home and join our team, serving patients in that office."

Established in 1966, Texas Retina Associates, with 14 offices throughout the state and 17 retina-fellowship-trained physicians, is Texas' largest, most experienced ophthalmology practice focused specifically on the diagnosis and medical and surgical management of diseases of the retina and vitreous. The practice's sub-specialized physician team has participated in more than 75 national clinical trials over the past 20 years, bringing the newest retina and vitreous treatments to its patients. To schedule an appointment with Dr. Christopher Fuller in Lubbock, call 806-792-0066. Learn more at www.texasretina.com.

MERGERS AND ACQUISITIONS

The medical marketplace continues to consolidate. From medical groups acquiring solo practitioners and other groups to large hospitals and health systems acquiring physician practices, medical group mergers and acquisitions are on the rise. The integration of operations and cultures in a merger or acquisition warrants its own chapter or even an entire book. Here, I want to focus on the critical communication components for this event.

1. **Create a comprehensive communication plan.** Think through all of the stakeholders involved—the physicians themselves, employees at both practices, patients, referring physicians and key community contacts. Timing and coordination are key, and you will have multiple layers and moving parts. See Exhibit 11.11 for a sample plan.

2. **Develop your messaging/story.** Help your audiences to understand why this merger is happening. Tell the story in your own words and do it as soon as possible. Share the benefits. Dispel any rumors.

3. **Create a Frequently Asked Questions (FAQ).** Think through all of the various questions that may arise from your stakeholders and the appropriate response for each. This document should be fluid and flexible as you will no doubt need to update it as you work through the process and encounter additional questions or concerns. Having a FAQ will help to ensure language and messaging that are consistent across the board.

4. **Communicate.** And communicate again. It is impossible to over-communicate during a merger or acquisition. Keeping people informed and providing answers and guidance will help to minimize any negative impact. Here are a few of the specific communication tools you may want to employ:

   • **Patient Letter.**—As with the other patient letters we have discussed, the goals are to inform in a timely manner and reassure. Highlight the benefits that will come with this new relationship but also be upfront about any changes that may impact them. If your accepted insurance plans will change, you will need to send a separate letter first to those patients who will be impacted. Let them know what is changing and when. Also enclose a list of all the insurance plans you will accept. See Exhibits 11.12 and 11.13 for sample letters.

- **Poster/Flyer.**—Make this piece a warm and friendly way to introduce your new affiliation and its benefits to your patients while emphasizing the same faces, service and quality care they have previously known.

- **Website and Social Media.**—Depending on the specific merger and which side of the affiliation you are on, you will either need to merge the content of your site with another's or accommodate information from another practice into yours. Be sure to work with your web firm to ensure a smooth transition from the old to the new. This will involve their expertise to minimize impact on your SEO and ensure proper redirection and navigation from the site that will be dissolving. And if your domain name will be changing, don't forget to update all of your printed materials. Be sure to craft a news story for the site about the merger and share on your social media channels.

EXHIBIT 11.11 Acquisition Marketing and Communications Plan

Background

The providers have great reputations and have been in practice for many years. This acquisition is part of a primary care growth strategy. The two physicians being acquired realized the need to be involved in a large group in order to remain successful in the changing healthcare environment.

Key Benefits/Messages

Need to assure current patients that:

- This will be a seamless transition. They do not have to do anything.
- Same office location and providers.
- They will remain their "neighborhood" doctors even though they are now part of a larger organization. It will not change the personal level of care patients are accustomed to receiving.
- This change will only enhance the level of care patients receive.

Key Benefits for Current Patients:

- Enhanced communication and access through an online patient portal available to you 24/7 so that you can request appointments and pay bills when it is most convenient for you as well as receive timely health information and updates.
- Improved care coordination.
- Increased access to specialists and specialty care, including the latest technology, medical advances and treatment options.

Key Messages:

- "Welcome to the Family".
- We're still in the same place with the same familiar faces you know and trust. Now, we're just part of a bigger family, allowing us to provide even more health resources for you and your family.

Tagline: "Good Health from Our Family to Yours"

PHASE 1: ACQUISITION COMMUNICATION (First 3 months)

Strategy	Notes
Internal	
Create a sign/poster on foam core to place in the office announcing that the practice is now a part of Physician Associates.	Headline: "Welcome to the Family" Assure them that they will receive the same level of quality, personal care they have known but now with greater access to additional resources (patient portal to reach us 24/7, network of specialists, etc.).
Create a flyer to make available throughout the office -- place in check in, check out, restrooms, waiting room, exam rooms, etc.	Flyer will mirror the messaging in the poster. Patients can take one with them if they would like. Need to train staff at desk to encourage patients to take one.
Write and send a letter to all of the practice's current patients.	Make this a personal, warm letter, signed by the docs, letting patients know about this exciting change and how it will make the practice even better. Reassure them that the physicians will continue to be their "neighborhood" doctor, providing personalized, quality care. Now they can do it even better.
Create bio/rack cards for the practice.	Try to make these personal and highlight what makes these providers special. Can be used as a handout at any talks or community events.
Need to ensure staff is trained not only in the new systems and protocol, but also equipped to answer questions from patients about his change. We can develop a frequently asked questions resource sheet to assist with this.	Ensure staff understands how this change will enhance the practice and care for patients.
Print blank note cards for this office with their names and the new logo.	Encourage the docs to use them to write personal thank-you notes to anyone who refers a patient to them.
External	
Website: Put up a "Coming Soon" announcement on the Physician Associates website now (home page banner). Draft all other content so ready to go live December 1 (bios, practice page/info., etc.)	
Write a news release about the acquisition and distribute to appropriate, targeted local media.	
Write and send a letter to key contacts/stakeholders outside the practice letting them know of the change.	Craft a letter similar to the patient letter that can go out to key community/professional contacts, colleagues and vendors.

EXHIBIT 11.12 Merger/Acquisition Patient Letter

Dear Patient:

Thank you for trusting us to care for you. We're excited to announce that as of December 1, 2013, we are joining the Physician Associates family. A part of Orlando Health, Physician Associates is one of the largest multi-specialty healthcare groups in Central Florida. This includes over 90 doctors practicing family medicine, internal medicine, pediatrics, obstetrics and gynecology, pediatric gastroenterology, orthopedics, podiatry and neuromusculoskeletal medicine.

We're still in the same place with the same familiar faces you know and trust. Now, we're just part of a bigger family, allowing us to provide even more health resources for you and your family, including:

- Enhanced communication and access through an online patient portal available to you 24/7 so that you can request appointments and pay bills when it is most convenient for you, as well as receive timely health information and updates
- Improved care coordination
- Increased access to specialists and specialty care from Orlando Health, including the latest technology, medical advances and treatment options

We truly value our relationship with you, and our goal is to make this transition as seamless as possible. Our focus has always been and will remain on providing you with the best healthcare to meet your individual needs. To learn more, we encourage you to visit the Physician Associates Web page at paof.com or call our office at 407-296-1923 with any questions.

Happy holidays and best wishes for good health from our family to yours!

Sincerely,

Scott D. Marsel, MD   Truc T. Tran, DO

EXHIBIT 11.13 Merger Patient Letter

Dear PATIENT NAME:

Thank you for trusting me to care for your eyes. I truly value our relationship and wanted to personally share some exciting news. Effective November 1, 2009, I will be joining Texas Retina Associates and serving patients in their Fort Worth office which is conveniently located just one-half mile west of my current office. My new address is:

900 W. Magnolia, Suite 205

Fort Worth, Texas 76104

817-334-0882

www.texasretina.com

Established more than 40 years ago, Texas Retina is the state's largest, most experienced ophthalmology practice focused specifically on the diagnosis, treatment and surgery of the retina and vitreous. I have always respected the physicians at Texas Retina, and we share the belief that eye care should be provided in a manner that is accessible, personal, attentive, professional and convenient to each and every patient we serve. Joining Texas Retina will ensure that I can provide you with access to the latest technology, medical advances and treatment options. In fact, Texas Retina has one of the largest clinical trials programs in the country for a non-academic practice. They are currently conducting 11 studies, testing promising new treatments for a variety of conditions, including both dry and wet age-related macular degeneration, diabetic retinopathy and uveitis.

I may be moving to a different office, but I want to assure you that I remain dedicated to you and all of the patients throughout Fort Worth whom I have had the privilege of caring for during the past 27 years. My focus has always been and will remain on restoring vision and providing you with the best possible eye care to meet your individual needs. My goal is to make this transition as easy for you as possible, and continuity of care is my top priority. As such, you can call 817-334-0882 to schedule an appointment with me after November 1 at Texas Retina's Fort Worth office. You may also call this number if you have an urgent eye care need before November 1, and I will make arrangements to ensure you receive the necessary medical attention. In addition, please take a moment to complete the enclosed form and mail it to the address listed above prior to coming in so that we can be sure to put this basic information in our database. And rest assured, we will also be able to acquire your medical records if necessary. Finally, I want to assure you that Texas Retina Associates accepts most insurance plans, and we will certainly verify that we accept your plan prior to your appointment. I hope to see you soon!

Best Regards,

Lee S. Anderson, MD

MOVING/OPENING A NEW OFFICE

There are few things that cause as much stress in a workplace as moving. It impacts your physicians, staff and patients alike. Handled improperly, it can do serious damage to **The Four A's—Access, Availability, Accountability** and **Accommodation**—causing disruption, frustration, confusion, anger and erosion of your patient base.

On the upside, moving and/or opening a new office can be an exciting time of growth, opening new doors of opportunity and enhancements to patient service and care. As with the other changes we have discussed in this chapter, the keys to a successful move or new office opening are proper planning and communication well in advance of the event. Here are some of the specific strategies you will want to incorporate into your plan:

1. **Inform and engage staff.** They are not only impacted personally and professionally by this change, they are also your front-line communicators with patients. Involve them in the planning process. Keep them informed of any changes. Seek their input and ideas. Empower them with the details and information they need to answer questions and ensure a smooth transition. This may include a frequently asked questions (FAQ), revised phone scripts and printed materials to share with patients.

2. **Update your website and social media.** Begin by placing a prominent banner or section on the home page of your site, announcing the move. Then, on the appropriate transition date, be sure to update and change all contact information on your site as appropriate. On your location and/or contact page, you can add an alert that as of a certain date, your office has moved. If you have practice profiles in other search or ratings sites, be sure to update your contact information there as well to reflect the move. And have some fun on your social media channels, providing photos and updates of any construction or even the move itself.

3. **Develop a phone strategy.** Find a way to incorporate information and reminders about the move into all of your phone conversations with patients regarding appointment reminders or scheduling. If your system has the capability, you can also add an on-hold message about the move.

4. **Ensure communication about the move throughout your office(s).** This can include posters, flyers and/or reminder postcards to hand patients at checkout. This might also be the perfect time to have a magnet

created that you can give patients at check-out so that they have a visible reminder with the new office contact information.

5. **Create a move announcement card or letter to mail to patients, referring physicians, vendors and friends of the practice.** Explain the reason for the move and the benefits it will provide to patients. When you include your new contact information, be sure to add way-finding or general directions with reference to any specific landmarks. See Exhibits 11.14 - 11.17 for examples.

6. **Send a news release to local community publications.** Depending on the significance of the move or new facility, this may generate a news story in your community. Flip back to Exhibit 8.1 for a news release we did for a big move by Texas Retina Associates along with the resulting media coverage in Exhibit 8.2.

7. **Get involved in your new neighborhood.** If your new office means a move to a new or different neighborhood, be sure to meet your new neighbors, using many of the strategies I outlined in Chapters 3 and 9. You may even want to hold an open house to invite friends and referral sources in to see the new facility. See Chapter 9 for additional details and ideas. As part of your opening, you could also consider making a charitable contribution to an organization or cause in your new neighborhood.

Moving is never easy, and it comes with a unique set of challenges for medical practices. However, with the right planning and coordination, and a solid communication strategy, it can place you on an exciting path for future growth and new opportunities. As Henry Ford once said, "If everyone is moving forward together, then success takes care of itself."

EXHIBIT 11.14 Sample Direct Mail Move Announcements

We're On the Move!
Announcing Our New Rockwall Office

To better serve you and your patients,
we're opening a new office in Rockwall:

2380 S. Goliad Street, Suite 120, Rockwall TX 75032
972-722-4739 • Fax: 972-722-4807

Opening August 19, 2015

- Scheduling advance appointments now: 214-692-6941
- After August 19: 972-722-4739

Deborah Y. Chong, MD

Ashkan M. Abbey, MD
*Joining our practice
September 1, 2015*

Texas Retina Associates

- Texas' **largest, most experienced** ophthalmology practice focused specifically on retina care
- **Sixteen retina-fellowship-trained physicians** highly skilled in diagnosis, treatment and surgery of the retina
- Participation in **national clinical trials** to bring our patients the newest treatments
- A reputation for personal, attentive, professional care **for more than 50 years**
- **Fourteen offices** throughout Texas to provide convenient patient access

www.texasretina.com

EXHIBIT 11.15 Sample Office Move Patient Letter

Dear PATIENT NAME:

Thank you for trusting us to care for your eyes. To better serve many of our patients, we are moving our Glen Rose office to Cleburne on March 11, 2013. The new office will be located at:

1665 Woodard Avenue

Cleburne, Texas 76033

817-334-0882

As you may know, we currently share our Glen Rose office with ophthalmologist Steve Surratt, MD. He recently opened a new office in Cleburne, and we will share it with him. Drs. Anderson and Beasley will continue to serve our patients in this new office.

With this new office location, along with our other 12 offices throughout the region, we remain Texas' largest, most experienced ophthalmology practice focused specifically on the diagnosis, treatment and surgery of the retina and vitreous. As a result, you can rest assured that one of our physicians is always on call to meet any urgent needs with instant access to your medical records through our electronic medical records system.

Most importantly, we care about you and want to assure you that we remain committed to meeting your individual needs and providing you with the most advanced, personal, attentive, professional and convenient care. To that end, we will do everything we can to ensure you experience a seamless transition to our new Cleburne office. We have enclosed a map, and it is also available on our website at www.texasretina.com.

If you have any questions or need to schedule your next appointment, please don't hesitate to call us at 817-334-0882.

Warmly,

Physician Name, MD

EXHIBIT 11.16 Sample Office Move Patient Letter

Dear Patients and Friends,

For the past several years, I have had the privilege to care for patients in the communities surrounding both my Edgewood and Lee Vista offices. I appreciate the trust you have placed in me and look forward to continuing to serve as your physician for years to come.

I have recently been given the opportunity to **relocate my Lee Vista practice** to Physician Associates' new Lake Nona office effective April 27, 2015:

9679 Lake Nona Village Place

Orlando, FL 32827

Phone: 407.245.1437

For my Lee Vista patients, the Lake Nona office is conveniently located just four miles south of my current Lee Vista office and can be easily reached via Narcoosee Road. I hope you will consider visiting me at my new location for your healthcare needs.

For my Edgewood office patients, I will continue to see you in the Edgewood office.

I'm taking new patients at both locations and would welcome referrals of your family, friends and neighbors. To schedule your next appointment, please call 407.245.1437. I thank you for your patience and support during this transition.

Warmly,

Daniel Goddard, MD

EXHIBIT 11.17 Office Move Referring Physician Letter

Dear Dr. NAME:

We are excited to announce that to better serve you and your patients, our Dallas office, along with our friends and partners at the Retina Foundation of the Southwest, are moving to a new, state-of-the-art, patient-centered facility in December 2012 located at:

9600 N. Central Expressway, Suite 100

Dallas, Texas 75231

214-692-6941

Together with the Retina Foundation, we have custom-designed this innovative facility from the ground up to offer easily accessible, academic-level care in the comfort of a community office setting, including:

- Immediate, expanded and direct access to breakthrough treatments and clinical trials for a full range of retina conditions through both Texas Retina Associates and The Retina Foundation of the Southwest

- Improved efficiency, reduced wait times and quicker lab results

- A centralized, convenient location at N. Central Expressway and Walnut Hill Lane

- Ample parking and easy access to our front door

With this new office location, along with our other 12 offices throughout the region, we remain Texas' largest, most experienced ophthalmology practice focused specifically on the diagnosis, treatment and surgery of the retina and vitreous. You can rest assured that one of our physicians is always on call to meet your patients' needs with instant access to their medical records through our electronic medical records system. In addition, our fellowship program continues to serve as a training facility for ophthalmologists sub-specializing in vitreoretinal care. This further enhances the level of care we are able to provide because as part of this program, our medical team is regularly reviewing and discussing the most challenging cases as well as the latest research and developments in our field, including emerging diagnostic tools and treatment methods.

As always, it is our true honor and privilege to work with you, and we remain committed to providing you and your patients with the most advanced, personal, attentive, professional and convenient care. Please feel free to call us anytime with your questions, comments or referrals – 940-382-1261.

Best Regards,

NAME, MD

CHAPTER 12

Tracking Your Results

So you've done your homework and developed your marketing plan. Now you're ready to begin implementing it. Before you begin launching specific strategies, there is one more step: How will you track the return on your investment (ROI) and know what is working?

Tracking marketing efforts for a medical practice is not an exact science. It is different than marketing for a specific product like a car. There is a complex web of factors that influence patients' decisions to select a specific physician which for many is a longer-term commitment. Some may be influenced by a single factor like a referring physician or family member while others respond after seeing information about your practice in a number of different places (that is why effective marketing plans include a layering of strategies and tactics). Not to mention that patients require different levels of care and resources, so from your end some may be a better target than others. All of these factors do not, however, mean tracking is impossible or should not be done. It will require planning, the right infrastructure within your practice and a little extra work on your end.

There are a number of ways to track your marketing efforts:

1. **Include a call to action.** On each marketing piece you produce—whether it be an ad, flyer, brochure, etc.—tell your audience what you want them to do. It can be to call, e-mail or visit your website. Include the phone number, e-mail address or website link. If you have the capability and want to take a more sophisticated approach, you can even designate a specific phone number, e-mail address or website landing page just for a specific marketing campaign. That way you know all of the

inquiries you receive on those specific channels are a direct result of your marketing efforts.

2. **Track calls and e-mails.** Make sure your staff members who answer the phones (or receive patient e-mails) are equipped to track the source of new patients. If someone calls to make an appointment for the first time, ask how they heard about the practice or who referred them. And ensure you have something set up within your computer system to easily document and track the response.

3. **Track referrals.** If you are a specialist, no doubt a large portion of your new patients come directly from physician referrals. Most EHR systems provide a way to track the source of each referral, but are you pulling reports and monitoring how many referrals you are receiving from each referring physician? Are you looking for trends so that you can thank those who have increased and check on those who may be declining? Make it a point to review this type of report monthly. If you are a larger group practice, do so for each physician individually in addition to looking at practice referrals as a whole. You will find this information invaluable as you target your marketing efforts using the strategies outlined in Chapter 3. If you are a primary care practice or want to take your tracking to a level higher, track non-physician referrals as well. You may learn that you have an "ambassador" patient who has sent 10 new patients your way in the last month. Certainly you will want to acknowledge and thank this patient either with a note or the next time you see him or her in the office.

4. **Track website traffic.** Google Analytics is a great, free service offered by Google to help you track who is visiting your website, which and how many pages they are visiting, click throughs for additional information, and how long they are staying on each page. I recommend reviewing your Google Analytics report on a weekly basis to determine which pages on your site are most effective, which ones aren't generating traffic or holding interest, and what may need to be changed to improve your results.

5. **Survey your patients.** While people don't always take direct action based on one specific marketing strategy, it still could have influenced their behavior. Create a brief "Where Have You Seen Us" checklist for your patients to complete during their visit. On it, list all of the places

you are currently marketing in the community—including ads, media stories, presentations, etc. Patients should be able to complete it quickly while they are waiting. Use this feedback as another tool to help evaluate the impact of your community marketing and public relations efforts.

6. **Develop and use reports.** Collecting data is great, but if no one is compiling and reviewing it regularly, it doesn't do you much good. Ensure that you are pulling reports at least monthly. Use technology to your advantage and find ways within your software system to pull the data you want and if possible, automate when and how often reports are produced.

7. **Take action.** Tracking and reports are worthless unless you take action based on the results. Determine which of your marketing strategies are working, which ones might need some tweaking, and which ones should be scrapped altogether. Look both short-term and long-term. Don't give up too early though. Some marketing campaigns take frequency and repetition before they stick. If possible, graph your results and look for trends. Are referrals trending downward for one of your steady referral sources? Give that physician a call as soon as you notice the decline to determine if something is wrong and take action to correct it.

Track your marketing efforts and take action based on the results, and you will stay a step ahead on the road to success.

CHAPTER 13

Final Words of Advice

As I asserted in the introduction to this book, successful medical group marketing today is all about understanding and effectively meeting the needs of your customers—whether they happen to be patients, referrers, staff, vendors, or others who interact with your practice. In other words, it means providing excellent customer service in each of **The Four A's—Accessibility, Availability, Accountability,** and **Accommodation.**

My aim is to provide a practical "how-to" guide that will allow you to implement effective marketing programs in your practice on your own or with the help of other professionals. Most measures I recommend can be implemented by almost any practice in the United States, no matter how large or how small.

In this book, I've gone a step beyond the basics. Although the basics are still important, particularly as they apply to building and maintaining your brand identity. That topic has been well covered by hundreds of books. This time, I've concentrated on customer service and the importance of building and nurturing relationships. This includes developing strong referral relationships, understanding your practice and the needs of your patients, engaging your staff to be marketers, telling your story through public relations and advertising, reaching out to your community, maintaining a strong online identity through your website and social media, and navigating your way through practice changes with skill and poise.

My ultimate goal is to help you develop and sustain a competitive advantage as you face the never-ending challenges of practicing medicine in today's environment. To that end, I've offered specific examples of actual plans, tools and tactics to illustrate how to accomplish my recommendations.

I hope I've helped empower you to take charge in your practice and, ultimately, your own destiny. I believe the secret to successful medical group marketing today is to understand what your patients/customers want and then find creative ways to provide it. Practices that can do this, along with delivering cost-effective, quality healthcare, are on a strong path to success and sustainability. Remember, satisfied customers are your best marketing tools of all.

About the Author

Andrea Eliscu, BS, RN, serves as President of Medical Marketing Inc., a healthcare marketing and public relations firm she co-founded in 1984. In this role, she provides leadership and guidance to clients throughout the country and also serves as a respected resource to local and national industry trade organizations and media on healthcare related issues. Throughout her career, Andrea has authored three books: *A+ Marketing: Proven Tactics for Success* as well as the popular *Ready - Set - Market!* and *Position for Success! Strategic Marketing for Group Practices*, all published by the Medical Group Management Association.

With a passion for community and the advancement of health and wellness, Andrea has devoted her leadership, creativity, and countless hours to a number of organizations, including, founder of the Orlando Dragon Boat Club, founder of the Dueling Dragons of Orlando ("cops and kids") dragon boat team, advisory board of BB&T Central Florida, board of directors of OneBlood, and board of directors of the Orlando Rowing Club. A graduate of Leadership Florida Class XIV, she also served on the Lt. Governor's Task Force for Education and was appointed a member of the WorkForce on Certificates of Need for the State of Florida. She previously served on the boards of the Florida Chamber of Commerce, the Healthy Florida Foundation, A Gift For Teaching, and Cornerstone Hospice. She also served on the Council of Governors of the MD Anderson Cancer Center, Orlando, and as an advisor to the College of Health and Public Affairs at the University of Central Florida.

Throughout her career, Andrea has received numerous awards and recognition for both her professional and volunteer achievements. These include the 2015 News 13 "Public Service Hero of the Year" Award; the 2015 "Golden Hands Award" from the Asian American Chamber of Commerce; a 2015 WKMG "Getting Results" award; the 2013 Health & Fitness Honoree for the "Women's Achievement Award" from the Women's Executive Council; a "Good Citizenship Award" from the

Orlando Police Department in 2012, 2013 and 2015; the 2011 National Philanthropy Day "Outstanding Volunteer Fundraiser" Award from the Central Florida Chapter of Fundraising Professionals; and the 2011 "Woman of Distinction" Award in Health and Wellness from the Girl Scouts of Citrus Council. She was also a finalist for the 2007 "Women Who Mean Business—Business Owner of the Year" award by the *Orlando Business Journal* and Orlando Health.

For the last five years, Andrea has devoted much of her free time and talents to growing the sport of dragon boating in Central Florida and specifically, the Dueling Dragons of Orlando, a program she founded in 2011, to bridge the divide between inner city kids and police officers.

The mission of Dueling Dragons is to use this ancient sport to build trust and long-term mentoring relationships at a critical time in the lives of both cops and kids in some of the city's toughest neighborhoods. The program addresses gang prevention, racism, profiling, and lack of respect for authority while instilling the values of discipline, dedication, teamwork, respect and paying it forward. The first program of its kind in the country, Dueling Dragons is garnering national attention thanks to a recent feature story by the Today Show. In addition, Andrea was invited to deliver a live TEDx talk in September 2015 about her work with the program. That talk is now available at https://www.youtube.com/watch?v=MR0UySGMKsM.

Appendix

Samples of Additional Referring Physician Communication Collateral.

Exhibit 3.6 *Florida MD* **Magazine Article. March 2013**
Exhibit 3.7 TRA Announcement of New Doctor to Practice
Exhibit 3.8 White Paper: Perioperative Blood Management
Exhibit 3.9 Referring Physician Brochure: JLR Center for Pain Management

Exhibit 3.6 *Florida MD* Magazine Article: March 2013

MARCH 2013 • COVERING THE I-4 CORRIDOR

Jewett Orthopaedic Clinic
Focuses on Achieving Pain Management

Regional Nerve Block Essential to Improved Orthopaedic Surgical Outcomes
Jewett Orthopaedic Clinic Focuses on Achieving Pain Management

By Nancy DeVault

"With roots firmly planted in the Central Florida community, Jewett has served as an international innovator and leader in orthopaedic care for over 75 years."

— *Charles M. May, Chief Executive Officer, Jewett Orthopaedic Clinic*

The largest and most distinguished orthopaedic surgical group in Central Florida, Jewett Orthopaedic Clinic, has partnered with JLR Medical Group, Inc., to pioneer the use of regional nerve blocks for improved pain management and orthopaedic surgical outcomes. This collaborative program is not only enhancing patient care and recovery, but has also emerged as a national model that other groups are seeking to emulate.

It's been 77 years since Eugene L. Jewett, MD, opened the practice doors, yet Jewett's physicians still embrace and embody his founding philosophy to improve patient orthopaedic health by maximizing function and mobility, caring for bones, joints, tendons, nerves, and ligaments of the limbs and spine. The Winter Park-based practice now treats patients at eight primary office locations and two convenient care centers. Subspecialty services — including sports medicine, joint replacement, foot and ankle, spine, and hand and upper extremity — are provided through the expertise of 26 board-certified, fellowship-trained physicians in addition to physician assistants, accredited nurse practitioners, and a multi-disciplinary team of clinicians, rehabilitative specialists, and other instrumental healthcare professionals.

Inspired by his desire to help handicapped individuals, especially children, Dr. Jewett's passion produced a prestigious medical career that earned him accolades for pioneering orthopaedic advancements, including prosthetic equipment and groundbreaking treatment methods. His first notable invention, in the 1930s, introduced a light-weight back brace to replace previously cumbersome aids. As a result, the mobility and recovery of patients significantly improved. Following service work as a US Naval physician, Dr. Jewett perfected the Jewett Hip Nail which revolutionized treatment of hip fractures in the 1940s. The method, which presented success rates of 95 percent, remained the standard approach for decades. During the 1950s and 60s, Dr. Jewett expanded his influence through two additions: the formation of the Jewett Foundation -- an effort which funded education for physicians in South America, and the introduction of partnering orthopaedic physicians who excelled in various subspecialties, resulting in a comprehensive practice and approach to patient care.

Thanks to this approach and strategic physician expansion, the

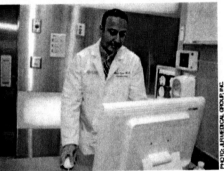

JLR Medical Group, Inc., anesthesiologist Moeed Azam, MD, has worked alongside Jewett Orthopaedic Clinic's Hugh Morris, MD, for years, using single injection nerve blocks for outpatient orthopaedic surgery. The program has since expanded to the hospital setting as well and includes post-operative pain catheters that slowly administer a nerve block remedy and can be dialed up or down as needed. This allows patients to receive anesthesia to a specific area for up to two to three days, decreasing breakthrough pain and helping them to jumpstart rehabilitation and recovery. The benefits of nerve blocks have revolutionized the outcomes of orthopaedic surgeries while significantly reducing the incidence of side effects.

Jewett Orthopaedic Clinic went on to become the first orthopaedic specialty practice in Florida to perform a total hip replacement (Charnley Low-Friction Arthroplasty) and the first to complete a total knee replacement in the Central Florida region. Additionally, Jewett Orthopaedic Clinic became well-recognized for designing and developing several innovative joint replacement systems used by orthopaedic professionals worldwide. In honor of Dr. Jewett's commitment to innovation, the Jewett Orthopaedic Clinic physicians continued to explore medical breakthroughs after his death and went on to perform many of Central Florida's first minimally invasive orthopaedic procedures, among other efforts, resulting in improvements to patient care, recovery periods and surgical outcomes.

The Center for Disease Control and Prevention reports that orthopaedic surgeries continue to rise and currently account for a significant portion of the 48 million inpatient surgeries performed annually in the United States. In 2009, the CDC announced that orthopaedic surgeons performed 676,000 total knee replacements and 327,000 total hip replacements within the previous year. Jewett Orthopaedic Clinic is poised to effectively treat the expected influx of joint replacement surgeries as a result of the aging "baby boomer" population.

EVOLUTION OF PAIN MANAGEMENT

With Jewett Orthopaedic Clinic for 25 years, Hugh Morris, MD, specializes in arthroscopic surgery of the hip and knee, hip and knee arthritis surgery, sports medicine, and joint replacement. Under his encouragement, Jewett worked to establish advanced pain management protocols with their physician colleagues at JLR Medical Group, the physician-owned, perioperative services company that administers anesthesia services and pain management for Jewett-led orthopaedic surgeries and minimally invasive procedures. The comprehensive surgical concept centered on the use of regional anesthesia, also referred to as regional nerve blocks, and the addition of continuous block catheters for maximized post-operative pain control.

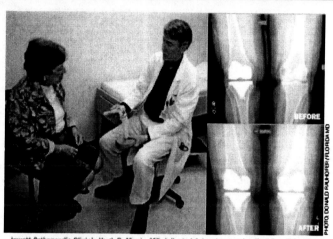

Jewett Orthopaedic Clinic's Hugh B. Morris, MD, talks to joint replacement patient June Krips about her new knee implant. Regional nerve blocks are enhancing quality of care for patients like Krips and improving surgical outcomes. In addition to pain management, this approach allows patients to begin rehabilitation sooner, improving range of motion, gait and balance.

As with any new endeavor, Dr. Morris admits to facing some initial challenges, but explains that the development of a nerve block program was essential to remain ahead of the orthopaedic medicine curve, as Jewett always has. As a result of this perseverance, Dr. Morris says, "Our pain management program is now one that is studied by other sites across the country."

Though Dr. Morris requested that nerve blocks be implemented for the sake of enhancing quality care of his patients, he credits two passionate anesthesiologists with delivering the complete strategy to introduce innovative protocols and train team members, including administrators, surgeons, pharmacists, nurses, and rehabilitation clinicians. He had extensive experience in single injection nerve blocks for outpatient orthopaedic surgery alongside anesthesiologist Moeed Azam, MD, Chief of Anesthesia for the Physician Surgical Care Center. Dr. Azam's partner, Thomas Looke, MD, Director of Research and Co-director of the Division of Regional Anesthesia and Acute Pain Management, translated the nerve block program into the hospital setting. About two years later, the program expanded to include post-operative pain catheters, including the ON-Q Pump, a small tennis ball-sized portable unit that slowly administers local anesthetic through a catheter.

"Regional nerve blocks allow us to provide anesthesia to the specified area of care for up to two or three days," explains Dr. Azam, who has practiced in Orlando for more than ten years.

Dr. Morris says that while no surgery is pain free, he views regional nerve block as the most significant improvement to anesthetic techniques in the last twenty-five years. Dr. Azam explains the timeline of succession, "In the 1980s, medicine introduced patient-controlled analgesia pumps (PCA); then in the 1990s, we saw the use of epidural pain control. Today, the multimodal regional anesthesia protocol addresses both the essential need for anesthesia during surgery and pain management. This is especially effective during total hip or knee replacement, or upper extremity surgeries such as shoulder reconstruction."

THE BUILDING BLOCKS OF NERVE BLOCK

Narcotics are potent pain relievers and were previously solely used as the standard of care for orthopaedic post-operative pain management. However, while narcotics effectively reduced pain levels, they posed a risk of complications and compromised safety for some patients.

With Jewett for 20 years, Brian Barnard, MD, an arthroscopic and reconstructive specialist of the hand, elbow and shoulder, shares the views of Dr. Azam and Dr. Morris. He believes that the benefits of nerve block have revolutionized the outcomes of orthopaedic surgeries while significantly decreasing the incidence of side effects.

After a pre-op nurse has completed traditional surgery preparations (including an IV), an anesthesiologist is likely to deliver local anesthesia as the first component in the protocol. For example, with upper extremity surgery, a numbing agent may be administered at the base of the neck; or for lower extremity, directed through a patient's thigh. Through a small needle, an ultrasound-guided nerve block catheter is inserted to allow anesthesia to be dialed into the specific region of nerves.

Types of upper extremity nerve blocks include supraclavicular block, axillary block, interscalene block, infraclavicular block, bier block, and wrist blocks. "We may also use general anesthesia or in some surgeries, the use of a spinal. This helps to make the patient comfortable and block pain, but also ensures that the patient remains still, which is essential since surgeons are working to execute precise techniques on small areas of the body," explains Dr. Barnard.

COVER STORY

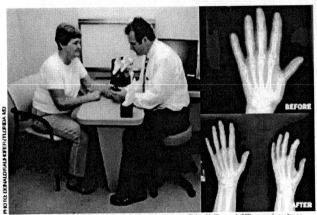

Jewett Orthopaedic Clinic hand, elbow and shoulder surgeon Brian K. Barnard, MD, examines Joyce Howell at her follow-up visit after recent hand surgery where a regional nerve block was applied. This approach blocks pain at every pathway, making the patient more comfortable during surgery. After surgery, patients are able to get the muscles working faster without significant pain, resulting in a quicker recovery.

Dr. Morris adds in reference to lower extremity nerve blocks, "We're able to block pain at every pathway — central nervous system, femoral, spinal, and local." Examples of lower extremity nerve blocks include lumbar plexus, sciatic, and femoral.

It benefits patients if they are alert following surgery, and devices like the ON-Q Pump, which can safely remain in place for days and be 'dialed up or down' as needed, eliminates the grogginess often associated with narcotics.

"This continuous nerve block instrument decreases breakthrough pain and allows patients, in some cases, to start same-day therapy and jumpstart rehabilitation and recovery," explains Dr. Barnard. He says regional nerve block is a vital component to the 180 total shoulder surgeries he completes annually, which account for approximately one-fifth of his surgical roster. He believes it is also critical to other total replacements such as elbow, wrist, or joints of the fingers, as well as minimally invasive procedures.

THE BENEFITS OF NERVE BLOCK

According to Dr. Azam, a major risk stemming from the use of narcotic-based pain management following a major operation such as hip and knee replacement surgery is the potential of developing Deep Vein Thrombosis (DVT) — blood clots usually formed in the legs.

"The risk of DVT is, in part, due to the patients' limited or complete lack of mobility. However, the continuous pain management of the ON-Q Pump now allows patients to get out of bed and start moving faster, so blood does not pool and swelling is minimized," explains Dr. Azam. He adds that it decreases side effects associated with narcotics, including urinary retention, postoperative delirium and cognitive dysfunction, respiratory problems, and other complications correlated to extended hospital stays such as infections and pneumonia. Additional advantages of using regional anesthesia and continuous block post-operative pain control catheters rather than narcotics include faster recovery rates, shorter hospital stays,

financial savings (patient and hospital), and elevated patient satisfaction.

Dr. Morris agrees that the reason regional nerve block has been such a 'medical game changer' for hip and knee replacement is because of the ability for patients to start moving safely sooner. "Patients are able to begin rehabilitation in-hospital earlier which then creates a better range of motion, improved gait and balance, and overall better surgical outcomes. There is something about treating the pain post-operatively that dramatically decreases the inflammation associated with healing."

As a result, Dr. Morris says his patients now achieve the same degree of healing and recovery at six weeks post-surgery, compared to previous patient outcomes (without nerve block) at the three to six month mark. "We're talking about a dramatic improvement in outcomes from just six years ago," he said.

Dr. Barnard echoes the impact on outcomes for upper extremity rehabilitation as well, "For shoulder repairs, the focus on initial motion is key. Therapists are able to get the muscles working faster without a significant level of pain." He proclaims that Jewett has been on the forefront of awareness and educating patients. "Many of my patients, especially those of the aging population, trust the established brand of Jewett and specifically schedule their procedures during their snowbird seasonal stay so they can benefit from the nerve block program and expertise of our team."

After completing thousands of joint replacement surgeries, Dr. Morris says better patient care is the bottom line. "I knew I wanted to be a doctor in the 6th grade," he shares. "Working in adult reconstructive surgery is extremely rewarding because you get to experience the appreciation of patients who may have suffered for years. Not only have surgical techniques improved, but surgical outcomes and recovery has vastly improved thanks to the use of nerve blocks and pain management."

ECONOMIC OUTCOMES

A study titled "The Economic Implications of a Multimodal Analgesic Regimen for Patients Undergoing Major Orthopedic Surgery: A Comparative Study of Direct Costs," which was published in the July-August 2009 issue of *Regional Anesthesia and Pain Medicine*, concluded the beneficial economic implications of regional nerve block. The article stated that, according to the US Healthcare Cost and Utilization Project, total knee and total hip replacement surgeries accounted for nearly $30 billion dollars in 2004, an increase of more than $9 billion dollars from the previous year. The authors indicated this was a result of the increased number of procedures being performed, which according to the American Academy of Orthopaedic Surgeons, will continue to rise as much as 50 percent per year for total hip arthroplasties and 300 percent for total knee arthroplasties through 2030.

The study was conducted on 100 patients receiving either to-book

magazine

tal knee or hip replacement at the Mayo Clinic. The economic comparison displayed results through three categories, including indirect, direct, and intangible costs. Indirect expenses included cost savings of lost productivity related to morbidity; and intangible cost savings related to pain and suffering. Most savings fell within the direct cost bracket, including physical supplies, labor, and time. "It is clear that the advancement of nerve block pain management has shortened hospital stays and therefore, generated a trickle effect of decreased costs," said Dr. Morris.

GETTING IN THE GAME OF ORTHOPAEDIC CARE

The Central Florida community boasts a number of professional and collegiate teams with athletes who risk sports-related injury. The Jewett Orthopaedic Clinic serves as the official team physicians for the NBA's Orlando Magic, the Arena Football League's Orlando Predators, teams at the University of Central Florida and Rollins College, multiple area high schools, and professional performance athletes, including the Orlando Ballet and Cirque Du Soleil.

"While an ideal surgical outcome and speedy recovery is a goal for all patients, nerve block techniques have been especially beneficial for elite athletes who require surgical interventions. Because of improved outcomes, we're able to get them back to performance faster," said Dr. Barnard.

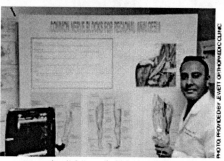

Jewett Orthopaedic Clinic physicians partnered with anesthesiologists at JLR Medical Group, Inc., including Moeed Azam, MD, to help introduce innovative pain management protocols using regional nerve blocks. The program addresses both anesthesia needs during surgery as well as post-op pain management, reducing negative side effects like Deep Vein Thrombosis (DVT) — blod clots usually formed in the legs, urinary retention, cognitive dysfunction and respiratory problems that sometimes result from the use of narcotics. It also helps reduce hospital length of stay and as a result, complications associated with extended hospital stays like infections and pneumonia.

With the addition of two Jewett Orthopaedic Convenient Care Centers in recent years, recreational sports enthusiasts and, of course, anyone in need of orthopaedic evaluation, can walk in for orthopaedic care such as broken bones, sprains, strains, and lacerations. Additionally, the availability of eight office locations makes patient care convenient, timely, and accessible. Charles M. May, Chief Executive Officer of Jewett Orthopaedic Clinic, explains that these developments are an extension of an overarching philosophy, "Throughout our history, Jewett has established high standards for customer-driven orthopaedic care. It is our mission to ensure that our patients achieve the best possible outcome."

JEWETT ORTHOPAEDIC CLINIC

EIGHT OFFICE LOCATIONS: Hours: Monday – Friday; 8:30 am to 5:00 pm

24-Hour Phone Service: Appointments (407) 629-2444 / Toll-free (800) 432-6635

Winter Park: (407) 647-2287 • 1285 Orange Avenue • Winter Park, FL 32789

Lake Mary – Stirling Center: (407) 206-4500 • 701 Platinum Point (off Rinehart Rd.) • Lake Mary, FL 32746

Orlando - Sandlake: (407) 345-1646 • 7300 Sandlake Commons Blvd. • Suite 127 • Orlando, FL 32819

Orlando - University: (407) 380-8705 • 3451 Technological Avenue, Suite 15 • Orlando, FL 32817

Orlando - Downtown: (407) 236-0404 • 1717 South Orange Avenue • Orlando, FL 32806

East Orlando: (407) 381-8441 • 7975 Lake Underhill Road, Suite 330 • Orlando, FL 32822

Maitland - RDV Sportsplex: (407) 916-4120 • 8701 Maitland Summit Boulevard • Orlando, FL 32810

Kissimmee/St. Cloud: (407) 593-2866 • 1931 South Narcoossee Road • St. Cloud, FL 34771

TWO JEWETT ORTHOPAEDIC CONVENIENT CARE CENTERS: Walk-In!

Monday - Thursday, 7:30 am to 8:00 pm • Friday, 7:30 AM - 4:00 PM • Saturday, 9:00 AM - 3:00 PM

1401 Minnesota Avenue • Winter Park, FL 32789 • (407) 599-3710

701 Platinum Point (off Rinehart Road) • Lake Mary, FL 32746 •(407) 206-4500

GET INVOLVED! Stay connected with innovation at JewettOrtho.com
Go social: facebook.com/JewettOrtho
twitter.com/JewettOrtho
youtube.com/user/JewettOrtho

JEWETT ORTHOPAEDIC CLINIC PHYSICIANS:

Brian K. Barnard, MD
Mark A. Beckner, MD
Joseph B. Billings, MD
Mary Lynn Brown, MD
John R. Chase, MD
Steven C. Choung, MD
Jeffrey A. Deren, MD
William Felix-Rodriguez, MD
Adam S. Fenichel, MD
Kurt A. Gasner, MD
Michael V. Jablonski, MD
Richard M. Konsens, MD
Kenneth A. Krumins, MD
Wadih S. Macksoud, MD
John W. McCutchen, MD
Sean M. McFadden, DO
Philip A. Meinhardt, MD
Ben Miller, MD
Craig M. Mintzer, MD
Hugh B. Morris, MD
Gregory O. Munson, MD
John A. Papa, MD
Janet M. Robison, MD
Richard L. Shure, MD
Reginald L. Tall, MD
Colleen M. Zittel, MD

Exhibit 3.7 TRA Announcement of New Doctor to Practice

Exhibit 3.8 White Paper: Perioperative Blood Management

PERIOPERATIVE BLOOD MANAGEMENT:
IMPROVING PATIENT OUTCOMES
AND REDUCING HEALTHCARE COSTS

devoted physicians.
collaborative partners.
metrics-driven quality.

jlrmedicalgroup.com

Perioperative Blood Management: Improving Patient Outcomes and Reducing Healthcare Costs

ANESTHESIA PARTNERS PROVIDE LEADERSHIP

March 2013

Healthcare reform is increasing demands on hospitals to achieve higher levels of quality, patient safety, efficiency and accountability. While reimbursements are shrinking, payor incentives are increasingly tied to evidence-based care and outcome measurements. Healthcare leaders are tasked with the challenge of identifying and rooting out "waste" -- defined by The New England Healthcare Institute as healthcare spending that can be eliminated without reducing quality of care. Premier healthcare alliance estimates that waste in the U.S. Healthcare system exceeds $1 trillion or nearly half of all healthcare costs.

Perioperative blood management, an evidence-based, multidisciplinary process designed to promote the optimal use of blood products throughout the hospital, directly addresses two of these unnecessary costs: resource over-utilization and avoidable complications. And anesthesiologists, because of their comprehensive role in preparing patients for surgery, reducing blood loss during surgery and directing care for patients post-operatively, can play a critical leadership role in the development and implementation of perioperative blood management programs.

Anesthesiologists: Operating Room Stewards

The Society for the Advancement of Blood Management defines patient blood management as the timely application of evidence-based medical and surgical concepts designed to maintain hemoglobin concentration, optimize hemostasis and minimize blood loss in an effort to improve patient outcomes. There are a number of strategies anesthesiologists can employ to achieve these goals from pre-op thru recovery. Since a majority of hospital patients enter the institution through the operating rooms, and the operating room has the lion's share of multi-unit transfusions, the anesthesiologists' role is critical. Oversight of preoperative assessment and patient optimization from integrated pre-op clinics is essential. Intraoperatively, techniques include sophisticated point-of-care coagulation monitoring with algorithm-guided transfusion therapy, controlled hypotension, warming and maintenance of normothermia, choice of ventilation patterns, choice of drugs, timing and amount of fluid administration, and choice of anesthetic techniques.[1]

In addition to their medical role, anesthesiologists increasingly hold valuable administrative responsibilities as well. Unlike the surgeons they work alongside, anesthesiologists do not have to split their time between the surgical suite and seeing patients in the office. They work day in and day out in the operating room. As a result, many hospitals are turning to their anesthesiology partners to manage operating suite resources, including the efficient use of operating rooms, equipment, supplies and personnel.[2] No one is more naturally aligned with the operating rooms' performance.

This combination of medical and administrative skills and experience uniquely positions anesthesiologists to provide leadership in hospital efforts like blood management that are designed to both improve patient outcomes and safety as well as enhance operating efficiency and reduce unnecessary costs.

Why is Perioperative Blood Management Necessary?

Transfusion practices vary greatly throughout facilities and across specialties for the exact same diagnosis and procedure, increasing over-utilization and exacerbating the challenges healthcare executives face. In one study Premier conducted of red blood cell use in 560 hospitals, transfusion rates in cardiac surgery varied from 10 to 100 percent per case. According to Premier, this occurs because physicians often rely on prescribing habits, using transfusions empirically to elevate blood counts rather than relying upon evidence-based guidelines that focus on clear indications and specific thresholds.

As a result of this variance, hospitals across the country are increasingly developing or expanding blood management programs to address these challenges. What typically started as a way to treat patients who refused transfusions, has evolved into an effort by hospitals to evaluate the necessity, outcomes and financial costs associated with transfusions.[3] Researchers have identified five primary drivers for the paradigm shift to patient blood management:[4]

1. The growing gap between supply and demand for blood products
2. The escalating cost of transfusion
3. Product safety issues
4. Adverse transfusion outcomes
5. Questionable efficacy of transfusions

In addition, the Joint Commission has adopted Patient Blood Management Performance Measures,[5] and The World Health Assembly, part of the World Health Organization, identified the need for patient blood management and passed a resolution adopting this approach at its 63rd session in 2010.[4]

Improving Outcomes and Patient Safety

Although the United States blood supply is safer today than ever before, transfusions carry risks. In fact, each unit of red blood cells transfused is associated with an incremental increased risk for an adverse outcome, including:

- An increase in morbidity and mortality
- Nosocomial infections
- Transfusion-related circulatory overload
- Higher financial costs
- Immunosuppression
- Transfusion-related lung injury
- Longer lengths of stay

In cardiac care, for example, red blood cell transfusion is *directly* associated with a risk-adjusted increased risk for every postoperative morbid event:

- Mortality (odds ratio [OR], 1.77)
- Prolonged ventilatory support (OR, 1.79)
- Cardiac complications (OR, 1.55)
- Renal failure (OR, 2.06)
- Serious infection (OR, 1.76)
- Neurologic events (OR, 1.37)

In an observational cohort study of 11,963 patients who underwent isolated coronary artery bypass from 1995 to 2002, of which 5,814 (48.6%) were transfused, each unit of red blood cells transfused was associated with an incrementally increased risk for adverse outcome.[6]

Meanwhile, studies show the clinical benefits of surgeries that avoid transfusions include lower infection rates, faster wound healing, shorter lengths of stay and fewer readmissions, just to name a few.

Blood Management Programs Save Hospitals Money

In addition to improving patient outcomes, blood management programs positively impact the bottom line. According to a study published in the April 2010 issue of the journal Transfusion, the cost of a red blood cell transfusion ranges from $522 to $1,183 per unit. This includes obtaining consent, screening, lab work, education and treating short-term side effects.[3] And in the U.S., approximately 15 million units of red blood cells are transfused every year according to the AABB (formerly the American Association of Blood Banks). Sherri Ozawa, R.N., board member for the Society for the Advancement of Blood Management and clinical director of the Institute for Blood Management at Englewood Hospital and Medical Center in New Jersey, estimates that about 90 percent or more of those 15 million units are provided to stable, non-bleeding patients.[3]

Adding to the direct and indirect costs, healthcare providers also increasingly face financial penalties for adverse clinical outcomes related to inappropriate transfusion practices. Medicare and most commercial health insurance carriers will not pay for transfusion errors, bleeding complications in cardiac surgery, and hospital-inquired infections that are increased significantly by blood transfusions.[7]

And when it comes to perioperative blood management, even small improvements can make a sizable financial impact. MedStar Georgetown University Hospital brought the first blood management program to the Washington, D.C., area in January 2011. Prior to that, the hospital had averaged about 1,200 units of blood a month. One of its orthopaedic surgeons, Mark Zawadsky, M.D., estimated that just reducing that amount by 10 percent resulted in an annual savings of about $750,000.[3]

Success Requires a Collaborative, Metrics-driven Approach

Critical factors for successful blood management programs include:

1. Measure and obtain an accurate comparison of utilization data.
2. Utilize a multi-disciplinary Blood Stewardship team to lead improvement efforts. Include anesthesiologists, surgeons, internists/hospitalists, family physicians, hospital administration, nursing, pharmacy and blood bank.
3. Work collaboratively with practitioners and identify physician champions.
4. Implement evidence-based transfusion guidelines and protocol-driven transfusion pathways.
5. Provide education and clinical decision support tools.
6. Develop a measurement and feedback process to monitor adherence to guidelines, track improvements and impacts, and communicate progress back to practitioners.

Many hospitals have also formed service-line focused blood management teams (i.e. cardiac surgery, orthopaedic surgery, etc.) to maximize efforts.

In the end, developing and implementing a comprehensive blood management program not only roots out "waste," improves hospitals' positions and directly addresses the key drivers of accountable care - it is simply good medicine.

About JLR Medical Group, Inc.

Founded in Orlando, Florida, in 1988 by Joseph L. Riley, MD, JLR Medical Group is a physician-owned, perioperative services company, providing anesthesia services and pain management throughout Central Florida. Its growing clinical team of 75 anesthesiologists and 120 nurse anesthetists perform over 100,000 cases per year. The company offers a complete, streamlined medical and management solution to achieve an optimally performing operating room.

JLR has established evidence-based transfusion guidelines for perioperative care and works with its clients to lead in blood management. One example of its recent efforts is the group's liver transplant program, which worked in partnership with surgeons and hospital leadership to achieve a better-than-average transfusion rate of under 5 units of blood per transplant during the first three years of the program. This was accomplished through intraoperative point-of-care coagulation analysis with thromboelastomery/thromboelastography as well as lower, more conservative transfusion triggers and algorithm-guided care.

REFERENCES

[1] Seeber, P., Shander, A., "Anesthesia -- More than Sleeping." Basics of Blood Management, Second Edition. 2013

[2] Lifeline to Modern Medicine. American Society of Anesthesiologists

[3] Frellick, M., "Better Blood Management Could be a Boon for Hospitals." Hospitals & Health Networks, September 9, 2012

[4] Hofmann, A., Farmer, S., Shander, A., "Five Drivers Shifting the Paradigm from Patient-Focused Transfusion Practice to Patient Blood Management." The Oncologist, 2011:16(suppl3):3-11

[5] http://www.jointcommission.org/patient_blood_management_performance_measures_project/

[6] Koch CG, et al, "Morbidity and Mortality Risk Associated with Red Blood Cell and Blood-component Transfusion in Isolated Coronary Artery Bypass Grafting." Critical Care Medicine 2006

[7] http://www.bloodmanagement.com/the-bloody-truth/the-bloody-truth

ADDITIONAL RESOURCES

Society for the Advancement of Blood Management
http://www.sabm.org

291 Southhall Lane
Suite 201
Maitland, Florida 32751
407.667.0444

jlrmedicalgroup.com

Exhibit 3.9 Referring Physician Brochure: JLR Center for Pain Management

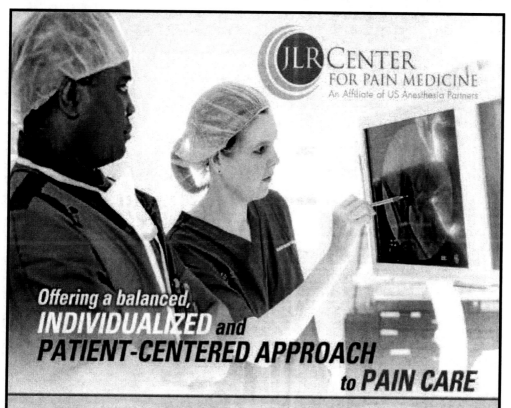

Offering a balanced,
INDIVIDUALIZED and
PATIENT-CENTERED APPROACH
to PAIN CARE

Each person's pain is different; so each patient care plan we create is individualized to maximize positive outcomes. These plans employ a variety of pain management strategies focused on the whole person — not just the pain.

Customized, Collaborative Care

- We believe in partnering with you to help care for your patients.
- Whether pain is post-surgical, acute or chronic, we truly believe the earlier a patient with pain is referred to us, the better their long-term outcomes will be.
- In many cases, through prompt, accurate diagnosis and early intervention, we can prevent acute pain from becoming a chronic problem.
- And throughout your patient's care, we pledge to keep you well informed on any treatments, medications or therapies we initiate.

"Pain is a universal experience but unique to each individual."
— Institute of Medicine (US) Committee on Advancing Pain Research, Care and Education

OUR MEDICAL TEAM

Skilled and experienced at treating even the most complex pain conditions, all of our physicians are board certified by the American Board of Anesthesiology with subspecialty certification in pain medicine. Several also hold certification from the American Board of Pain Medicine. Our physicians have consistently been awarded "Top Docs" by their local peers as seen in Orlando magazine.

Evans Amune, MD	D. Brian Jager, MD	Anand Patel, MD
Kayvan Ariani, MD	Suresh Kannan, MD	Rick Nieves-Ramos, MD
Jenny Chang, MD	Kacey Montgomery, MD	Michael Rubeis, MD
Diego Guerrero, MD		

Exceptional Training. Experienced Pain Care Leaders.

Our physicians have trained at some of the most respected universities and hospitals throughout the country.

Cedars Sinai Medical Center	The Ohio State University
Harvard University	University of Florida College of Medicine
Mayo Medical Center	University of Massachusetts Medical Center
National Institutes of Health	University of Miami Miller School of Medicine
New York Presbyterian - Cornell Hospital	University of Washington
Stanford University School of Medicine	Wake Forest University Bowman Gray School of Medicine

We also have a team of nurse practitioners who work closely with us to ensure your patients have greater access to the personalized care they need when they need it.

Cathy Behnke, MSN, ARNP	Holly Young MSN, ARNP, ACNP-BC
Eileen Delacova, MSN, ARNP-BC	Teri Boutty MSN ARNP-BC

A Balanced Approach

We also believe in taking a balanced and clinically-proven approach to treating both acute and chronic pain. This means we address the physical, emotional, social and psychological aspects of your patient's pain to achieve the best possible outcome. Components of a balanced pain management plan may include:

- minimally-invasive injection-based therapy
- psychological counseling
- medication
- physical therapy and rehabilitation
- social support
- other complementary approaches

Interventional Pain Management

We rely less on the traditional use of narcotic relief to simply mask symptoms and instead focus on establishing the underlying diagnosis to better direct future treatments. To help accomplish this, we employ safe, effective, minimally invasive procedures that can provide substantial diagnostic information and open up avenues for long-term relief.

Examples include:

- epidural steroid injections
- radiofrequency denervation
- selective nerve blocks
- neuromodulation (spinal cord stimulation)

Placing a Priority on Patient Satisfaction

- Friendly, attentive staff
- Caring providers
- Prompt availability for scheduling appointments
- Easy access when your patients need to reach us with questions or concerns

"I have had the privilege to work with JLR pain management physicians for the past five years, and they consistently provide the highest level of pain management care available in Central Florida. Whenever I refer a patient, I can rest assured that they will receive timely, compassionate, and appropriate care. I have witnessed countless excellent outcomes from JLR's interventional pain procedures."

— Philip Mainhardt, M.D. -Spine Surgeon - Jewett Orthopaedic Clinic

"I have been very content and pleased sending my patients to the JLR Center for Pain Medicine. I appreciate their approach in treating the whole person and empowering their patients with tools to manage their pain. JLR provides exceptional care using best practices, and they are my preferred provider of choice for referrals. My patients have praised their compassion while maintaining an efficient office and are thankful for medication samples, coupons and other cost-saving options. Despite their busy practice, JLR Center for Pain Medicine physicians are able to see my patients promptly."

— Anil Patel, M.D. - Family Medicine - Physician Associates

PAIN CONDITIONS WE TREAT

We are experienced and trained in a full range of minimally-invasive diagnostic and pain treatment options for acute, chronic and complex pain conditions, including:

- Facial/Head Pain
- Neck/Shoulder/Arm Pain
- Mid-back Pain
- Lower Back/Buttock/Leg Pain
- Joint Pain — Hip/Knee/Shoulder
- Cancer Pain
- Nerve Pain

One of our goals is to minimize the risk of opioid hyperalgesia that often occurs when opioids are the sole treatment modality offered to patients or doses are utilized beyond what is medically appropriate. Our ultimate goal is to provide long-term relief and get your patients back to enjoying life.

A HISTORY of
CLINICAL LEADERSHIP and INNOVATION

Named after Joseph L. Riley, MD, and founded in Orlando, Florida, in 1988, JLR Medical Group is one of Florida's largest physician-owned anesthesia practices, providing both anesthesia and pain management services throughout Central Florida. JLR recognized the emergence of the field of pain management as its own specialty and also foresaw an increasing need for physicians with specialized training and skills dedicated solely to caring for complex pain conditions. In 2007, JLR established its Center for Pain Medicine division.

Founding Partner of U.S. Anesthesia Partners

In January 2104, JLR Medical Group became a founding partner in U.S. Anesthesia Partners, an anesthesia-focused physician services organization. This has allowed our physician team to collaborate with other leading anesthesia and pain medicine groups, sharing best practices, improving our collective clinical performance, and increasing the level of service we can provide to our patients.

US ANESTHESIA PARTNERS

Our
LOCATIONS

Altamonte
711 E. Altamonte Drive, Suite 100
Altamonte Springs, FL 32701
Phone: 321-422-7111
Fax: 407-667-0140

Celebration
400 Celebration Place, Suite A340
Celebration, FL 34747
Phone: 321-422-7111
Fax: 407-667-0140

East Orlando
7727 Lake Underhill Rd.
Orlando, FL 32822
Phone: 321-422-7111
Fax: 407-667-0140

Ivanhoe Village
2501 N. Orange Ave., Suite 331
Orlando, FL 32822
Phone: 321-422-7111
Fax: 407-667-0140

Lake Mary
3300 W. Lake Mary Blvd., Suite 330
Lake Mary, FL 32746
Phone: 321-422-7111
Fax: 407-667-0140

Orange City
1601 Medical Center Drive, Suite 201
Orange City, FL 32763
Phone: 321-422-7111
Fax: 407-667-0140

Sandlake
7350 Sandlake Commons Blvd., Suite 1115
Orlando, FL 32819
Phone: 321-422-7111
Fax: 407-667-0140

Villages
1400 US Hwy. 441 N., Suite 536
Villages, FL 32159
Phone: 321-422-7111
Fax: 407-667-0140

Winter Park
2056 Aloma Ave., Suite 101
Winter Park, FL 32792
Phone: 321-422-7111
Fax: 407-667-0140

JLR CENTER
FOR PAIN MEDICINE
An Affiliate of US Anesthesia Partners

Phone: 321-422-7111
Fax: 407-667-0140

centerforpain.com

Index

CPSIA information can be obtained
at www.ICGtesting.com
Printed in the USA
FFOW01n1659181016
28596FF